Dying to Meet Them

One Woman's Incredible Journey from N.D.E. to U.A.P.

Mindy Tautfest

Foreword by

Teri Lynge – Kehl

Dying to Meet Them

One Woman's Incredible Journey from N.D.E. to U.A.P.

Mindy Tautfest

ISBN: 979-8-9887888-0-5

Printed in the United States of America

Cover design and synopsis by JJ Tautfest

Un-X Media Publishing
A division of HearthMasters, Inc.
PO Box 1166
Independence, Missouri 64051
www.unxmedia.com

Endorsements

"Mindy Tautfest's brilliant work of nonfiction transports readers on a fascinating journey through her life as a Near-Death Experiencer and beyond. She launches a new avocation as a Ufologist for the Mutual UFO Network and becomes MUFON Oklahoma's State Director and Dean of MUFON University. Through investigation and research, she learns that ET contact experiences and NDEs accelerate paranormal activity, psychic awareness, spirituality, altruistic feelings, synchronicities, etcetera. She ponders the true nature of reality and the scientific hypotheses of those who specialize in these fascinating fields of study. If you are looking for an uplifting page turner, go no further."

Kathleen Marden
Author of *FORBIDDEN KNOWLEDGE: A Personal Journey from Alien Abduction to Spiritual Transformation*

"The book Dying to Meet Them is Mindy Tautfest's account of her Near-Death experience and after-effects which are truly remarkable. Mindy explains that like many NDE experiencers, she now has a heightened awareness of the world around her and has remarkable encounters with inter-dimensional beings and personal experiences that go way beyond the norm. I highly recommend this unique book to anyone looking for answers to questions that go beyond our 3-D reality."

Margie Kay
Author, publisher, and president of the KUNX Digital Broadcasting Network

Dedication

For John, JJ, and Aneshka.

Your love brought me out of the darkness, and it will eternally remain the most important thing I have ever had the privilege to encounter.

Thank you.

Foreword

To know Mindy is simply to love her! I met her back in 2021 while visiting an online Zoom meeting for MUFON, (which is the acronym for the "Mutual UFO Network") State Directors. Being one of the National MUFON Board of Directors and a former MUFON State Director myself, I enjoy staying in touch and in tune with all the current State Directors, and this evening was no different. There were all these little squares with each person's face in the meeting on my computer screen and Mindy just stood out, it was like she was a friend I had known all my life, and she was just there, suddenly, in that little square. Somehow, in that very moment it was as if I chose to work with her, get to know her, be her friend, like it was always meant to be.

And so, it was! I contacted her within the week, and we spoke on the phone for six hours. Like we were catching up from being separated through time and space a hundred years. I found out in that time she and I had lived very similar lives just in our own personal, different ways. There was so much energy in our conversation that day it was hard to hang up. We became close friends in those 6 hours and have worked together ever since.

We spoke frequently and ufology was our passion. There was updating and new criteria to be handled and I felt like Mindy truly "got me." She understood the need and possessed the wherewith-all to make it happen. We rolled up our sleeves! Mindy shared with me that she had been through so much with her debilitating aneurysm and her near death experience, but she had the courage to go after her dreams and turn this unfortunate mental and physical battle into a positive lesson which made an incredible impact on her life, and on the lives of all who knew her. Even though it changed her life and the way she looked at everything, both mentally and spiritually, it was a powerful experience. It led her onto new avenues of thought and life! Her NDE (Near Death Experience) she shared with me was completely different from my own NDE, and we kept comparing notes about it, over and over. Asking why? How? What were the reasons and where were the answers to these experiences?

Mindy was gripped with the results of her NDE. She suffered physically and for so long, where was GOD? Where was her Light at the end of the tunnel? Where was the Happiness she heard so many others talk about while experiencing their NDE? While sharing my own NDE with her, she found that although mine was everything she was looking for in her own experience, it was nothing like what she had experienced! It drew us even closer as friends.

Being a thorough investigator, Mindy took on the challenge to find her answers. Our friendship took on new levels as we spent hours talking after the fact, looking into the "how" and "why" behind life presenting these conundrums. It was such a painful adventure for Mindy, one has to wonder, what does it all mean? From these moments we shared a bond talking about what she lived through, and I felt as if she was a sister from another mother, as we could almost finish each other's sentences!

Mindy has been so dedicated to overcoming the pain and suffering she experienced from her NDE. Her experience brought physical changes to her body and her life. Her family was so traumatized by almost losing her and she became so fragile through it all that the family was separated to allow her better care and comfort. She had been on a whirlwind life-changing journey and was living each day as if it was her last. She had felt as if her life had not been fulfilled, what was life all about? Then one day hanging onto faith, or perhaps sheer determination to experience something new before she left this life, she decided to visit Roswell, a bucket list moment, and the rest was history.

This book is so well written, and Mindy pours her heart out about all her fears and challenges. Living through the Void, the days of hardships and revelations which kept on for so long, it broke my heart to hear of all her suffering. Her love for her family which motivated her on, and her love for MUFON, brought her out of her pain and suffering, slowly, one month at a time until she found new footing for her future. Becoming a State Director, speaking about one of her cases at a MUFON Symposium, and on to Alien Con and Ancient Aliens on the History Channel. Her accomplishments took off and her light burns brightly.

Grab a cup of tea, sit back, and enjoy her journey. I cried with her as I read all she suffered and laughed with her as she found her resolve with it all. Mindy is an overcomer with a delightful attitude and outlook on life, she is just beginning her journey in Ufology, and I could not be prouder of her.

Teri Lynge-Kehl

Contents

Preface

I have heard it said that truth is oftentimes stranger than fiction, but little did I know just how strange the events about to unfold in my life would turn out to be. My journey into a world of strange new truths began on Tuesday, November the 18th, 2016 with a chance encounter for which I could have never prepared. One might recognize the day as the date of one of the most anticipated and heated US Presidential elections in recent history. Passions were high on both sides of the aisle as record numbers of voters turned up to cast their votes which would decide the direction of our country for the next four years. It was amid these national tensions that I found myself sitting in our old rundown trailer house located in the endless wheat fields of Northern Oklahoma. This emotionally charged atmosphere and humble setting is where I had come to draw my last breath at the age of 36.

At the time of this writing, it has been six years since that fateful day when I was unexpectedly whisked away from the happy life I had built together with my husband and children. In an instant, I found myself alone, plunged into a world of darkness with little hope of ever escaping my newfound dwelling place. Unbeknownst to me at the time, I would emerge from the unbidden journey bearing the great and terrible scars which would serve to lead me on a path of healing and discovery. My trauma, fears, anguish, and sorrows have in time transformed into a deeper appreciation for the nature of our existence in general, as well as a fascination with the function of our time on this Earth.

The purpose of this book is not to convince you that what I experienced is real. I know that it is, and you will know that it is real once you embark on your own journey into the afterlife. Instead, my purpose, in part, is to inform this ambivalent world that there is a place commonly known as the Void which exists on the other side of this life. You may very well find yourself there upon the occasion of your own death, and if you do, my hope is that you will have at least an ounce of comfort knowing that others have visited this place... A few have even traversed the dark abyss and lived to tell its secrets.

Disclaimer

As I was nearing the end of writing this book, I was sitting on my couch one day searching Netflix for a show to watch while I answered some emails. I decided to settle on a short documentary series titled "Sins of Our Mother" which focused on the mysterious disappearance of two young siblings from Idaho in 2019. Tylee Ryan, aged 16, and J.J. Vallow, aged 7, were both later found buried in shallow graves on the property belonging to their mother, Lori Vallow, and her new husband, Chad Daybell. At the time of this writing, Daybell and Vallow have been found competent to stand trial which is currently scheduled to begin in late 2023.

Several mysterious deaths surrounded the couple following Daybell's own Near-Death Experience during a swimming accident. Crediting his NDE, he later claimed that he was able to tell who was of the light and who was full of darkness, even going so far as to say that he was able to discern those who had become soulless and had turned into zombies. Hearing the story behind their twisted beliefs, I only felt it prudent to include a word of caution to those who may be reading this book, or any book within the NDE or UFO genre, in an attempt to glean deeper spiritual insights. The Daybell/Vallow case is an extreme example of the harm that can be done by those in the NDE or UFO communities claiming to have special revelations from God or from other ascended beings.

Although we are able to scientifically prove that some of us have suffered temporary death states, there is currently no objective way to validate anyone's Near-Death Experience. This being the case, literally anyone can claim to have had this type of experience in order to further their own agenda for obtaining power, fame, or financial gain. Some now even claim to have had similar NDE type experiences through practices such as mediation, or even from just having the experience of being afraid that they might die. While some of these encounters may be valid, many of these "NDE- like" experiences have served to open the door further to those who may seek to deceive the NDE community for their own gain.

I urge the reader to be critically discerning and exercise extreme caution with anyone trying to force their teachings or specific brand of belief as the only way to obtain spiritual enlightenment and understanding. Even my own story should be taken for what it is, a very personal experience which served as a transformative event in my own life, as well as in the lives of those closest to me. That said, I do not endorse the use of my story or experiences to support or discredit any one religious view or scientific hypothesis since I feel that what I experienced during my NDE is something that is meant for all of mankind. It is my belief that every single one of us will have our own encounter upon our passing where we will finally rest in the full knowledge of our wondrous existence. Until then, special care should be taken when determining what truths we choose to take from awe-inspiring yet unverifiable claims.

Chapter 1

The Beginning of the End

"Sometimes you get to what you thought was the end, and you find it's a whole new beginning."

- Author Anne Tyler

It was the Summer of 2016 when we moved out to the family farm to help my Father-In-Law tend to more than 300 acres (about half the area of Central Park in New York City) of wheat crops and multiple head of cattle he had at the main pasture. It was quite a large undertaking for a man in his 70s. I know he was happy to have John back at his side to help with the harvest and to lend a helping hand when the combine or other large farm machinery needed fixing. John had grown up on the farm along with his two sisters and none of them were strangers to the hard work which the lifestyle demanded. The Tautfest family had farmed the land and raised their children on that same patch of earth for five generations, if counting our own little ones. John's father lived at the main home site, but with no available homes in the surrounding area, our only option was to move into a small trailer house which we rented from the neighbors across the street until we were able to build a new family home on the Tautfest land.

1

At the time, both of our children were elementary age, and we were excited that they would be able to attend the same rural school which John had attended as a child. He often shared a story about the school lunch lady calling him "Little Rex", a nod to how closely he resembled his father whom she had served school lunches to when he was a child. We giggled at the thought that she may still be there in her unchanging form ready to welcome our son with a heaping spoonful of mashed potatoes and a comment about how much he looked like his grandfather. At eight years old, JJ was almost always running full force wherever he went. He had the biggest blue eyes and the deepest dimples you could imagine on a child with a belly laugh that could bring a smile to the sternest adult. Following close behind him on any given day, you could find our sweet six-year-old Aneshka. She has always had a gentle nature and quiet wisdom about her, but it was also well known that she would not put up with any guff from her older brother. She thrived being brought up in an environment surrounded by all the farm animals and would attempt to give the biggest hugs and snuggles to all that she encountered.

When we met in 2006, John had been working as the lead pastor at a Disciples of Christ church in northern Oklahoma. Throughout our marriage, he had taken different jobs to support our family but had almost always maintained a pastoral position at various churches within the Christian faith even if only in a bi-vocational manner. He also held a teaching license and most commonly would work at the local school teaching history and coaching basketball throughout the week while Sundays were reserved for delivering sermons from the pulpit. Once we had relocated to the farm, his schedule stayed quite busy with repairing equipment and tending to the daily chores, so he chose to focus on teaching at the local school to earn a living.

Both of us being brought up in Christian homes, we were a deeply religious couple, and we raised our children to know Jesus as their Lord. Our faith was at the center of all we did, and we regularly prayed and did Bible studies together as a family. Although John was not preaching each Sunday, we stayed active in the church and became members at the Baptist church in a neighboring small town. We enjoyed attending service at our new home church since the pastor and his wife were young and had children around the same ages as our own. I very much appreciated the slower pace of country life which afforded time for fellowship with our friends as well as plenty of quality time to spend with the family while putting in a hard day of work out in the field.

My childhood had been spent amid the hustle and bustle of Oklahoma's capital city, and I was used to a much faster pace of life than the one I was currently enjoying. I found that the farm offered a nice balance of hard work and leisure that my life previously had been lacking. At the age of 19, I had earned my certification as a Licensed Practical Nurse and went to work at the Intensive Care Unit of one of the smaller independent hospitals in the city. I enjoyed caring for others and thrived while working in an environment which required a coordinated team effort for treating those on the unit. The concentrated setting allowed me the ability to better understand the needs of my patients and their families, and I found that it helped with administering the appropriate care at a moment's notice. After several years at one hospital, I decided to take a new position working for a nursing agency which contracted with multiple hospitals in the area. While it afforded the freedom to travel between different hospitals and different related specialties, my primary focus always remained around ICU work.

With the valuable experience I had gained over the years working such diverse jobs within the nursing field, I soon found myself taking on the exciting adventure of employment as a travel nurse. Being young and single at the time, I thoroughly enjoyed taking various three-month assignments in different states across America. I would often accept positions in states where friends were currently living, and I would visit with them between workdays to explore the area and take in local attractions. After a ninety-day assignment was completed, I would return to Oklahoma to rest and await the next available assignment destination. Oftentimes I would stay active while home by volunteering with the Southern Baptist Disaster Relief and the Medical Reserve Corps. Anyone living in Oklahoma for any amount of time can attest to the fact that we are no strangers to the devastation that severe weather can bring to our hometown without a moment's notice. After any big flood or fire, I stayed quite busy working mud-out and ash-out duty alongside some of the most amazing, selfless, and dedicated men walking on this earth. Our teams would be called in to remove ash or debris after a natural disaster and help set the homeowner on a course to recovery. This often involved the back-breaking work of shoveling and sifting tons of debris to help locate any missing heirloom items important to the homeowner, or removing drywall from a home that was overrun with mold after a flooding event. When tornadoes struck, I would be activated in my nursing capacity to work triage, pre-op or any other position that was needed to help treat the flow of victims pouring into the local hospital. Luckily, the real big ones do not hit very often, and I only got called to respond a handful of times.

It was during one of my return trips home from a travel assignment on the east coast when I met John and fell head over heels in love with him. From his parsonage in a small community north of the city, he had written a short note to me on Myspace hoping to connect. At first, I passed him by, and his note got lost in the mix of other messages I had received through the website. Luckily for me, he was persistent and wrote another, much longer letter a few weeks later. This time his message caught my attention, and I quickly wrote back to invite him out for a friend's birthday celebration that night. It was St. Patrick's Day and there were festivities taking place in Oklahoma City's downtown area known as Bricktown. The streets were lined with people celebrating the holiday and decked out in their best green attire. I can still remember receiving the text message from him letting me know he had arrived in the area. I quickly ran towards the direction from which he was approaching, and once my eyes locked with his, I was instantly taken. We closed down the town that night before heading over to a friend's home and talking until the sun came up. If there was ever love at first sight, then this was certainly it.

After that first evening together, John and I were inseparable. In our whirlwind romance, we moved into a new home together after two weeks of dating, became engaged after six weeks, and were married by the end of the year. I continued working through the local nursing agency after becoming engaged, but soon moved my license to inactive status after becoming pregnant with our first child. I suffered a rough pregnancy due to bleeding problems and I was put on bed rest restrictions for most of the second and third trimesters. At the time, I did not know I had an underlying condition which made this pregnancy a high risk and was the cause of the uncontrolled bleeding. Nevertheless, I followed my doctor's advice precisely and remained on strict bed rest until my due date. In June of 2007, after 2 days of labor, I delivered our son JJ who arrived "sunny side up" and in fetal distress. After a team worked to clear his lungs and get him breathing, it was determined that he was perfectly healthy, and he was sent home from the hospital with us two days later.

Working as a stay-at-home mom was something that I had aspired to do ever since I was a little girl. Within two years of having our son, our daughter Aneshka was brought into this world. My heart felt so complete and content with the treasured little family we had created. I loved being home with my children and having that time to bond with them while they were so young. I found it incredibly rewarding to pour myself into teaching our children basic life lessons during their most formative years.

John received a job offer preaching at a Southern Baptist church in Eastern Oklahoma near Lake Tenkiller shortly after Aneshka was born. We bought our first home on the golf course that bordered the lake and went to work personalizing it for the kids. We painted JJ's room with murals of space, while Aneshka's room was themed to look like a beautiful butterfly garden. We had a humongous deck out back that overlooked the valley below and we would often roast marshmallows in the outdoor fireplace during warm summer nights. Most of our days were filled with taking the kids hiking in the surrounding woods, swimming in the lake, or fishing for channel cats from the shore. We loved our home on the lake and we lived there for five years until my father-in-law's health began failing. Sticking to the policy that family always comes first, we sold our lake home and moved up north when it became apparent that he needed John's help to maintain the family farm.

In the end, the arrangement to move back to the farm worked in our favor as well. It was nice to be closer to family once again, and to be perfectly honest, my health was not doing so great lately either. The first hints of my health problems had been evident from a very young age. When I was born, it was found that I had an extra rib on the right side of my ribcage which protruded under my skin and made my abdomen appear somewhat misshapen. As a child, I was diagnosed with scoliosis, and I often found it hard to keep up with the other kids physically. It is safe to say that I was never one to reach the top of the rope in gym class or to produce even one chin up. I can still remember the embarrassment I felt as my second-grade gym teacher waited impatiently watching as I struggled to lift my chin over the bar. Try as I might, all I could do was dangle helplessly below it. Taking some pity, she finally resorted to grabbing my legs and physically lifting me above the bar so she could mark it off as complete.

Once I hit my teen years, new symptoms began to appear, and old ones continued to worsen. I was always covered in bruises, and I started getting lightheaded with the slightest change in position. I would often nearly faint, catching myself just in time to prevent dropping to the floor. The unrelenting and unexplained pain I felt throughout my body was overwhelming. When alone, I would often cry from the frustration I felt living with such pain. I began getting migraines that would cause a temporary loss of vision and would result in being stuck in bed for days. Despite all of this, I hid my ailments well and outwardly led a relatively normal life. I danced in the high school pom squad, sang in show choir, performed in community theater, applied myself academically to my honors courses, attended vocational technical school to obtain my nursing degree, and worked part time as a carhop in the evenings. Every Wednesday and Sunday, one could find me attending a youth group at the Baptist church down the road. I stayed rather active during my teens, and I believe the fact that I was able to "suck it up" and press through my pain resulted in doctors mostly shrugging off my complaints if not outright just dismissing them altogether.

After I had graduated high school and began my nursing profession, I chose to work the night shift to earn more money. On the Intensive Care Unit, shifts were only offered in twelve-hour increments, so I found myself working 7 pm to 7 am at least three nights a week. I didn't realize it at the time, but this schedule played havoc on my already strained body. After six years of working night shifts at hospitals across the United States, I started falling. The first couple of times I just tried to laugh it off as if I was just being clumsy. I was only twenty-five years old and felt I had my whole career and a life full of opportunities ahead of me. But after taking a rather hard tumble on the unit one night, I realized that this was more than just simple clumsiness. My legs had randomly started going numb from the waist down and I knew that something was terribly wrong with my body.

Over the next few years, I began visiting different specialists in an attempt to find some answers as to what had been ailing me since birth. Various doctors had offered a range of different possible diagnoses. Chronic Fatigue Syndrome, Fibromyalgia, Probable Multiple Sclerosis. None were a definitive diagnosis. My condition had continued to deteriorate after giving birth to my children and it only served to confirm my need to take a step back from my nursing career. It was not an easy thing to do because I loved my profession. By the time the kids were entering school, I was having trouble eating, I was lightheaded most of the day, I would get terrible migraines, and my body hurt all the time. On particularly bad days, I would wince from the pain of our kids attempting to crawl into my lap, and then I would cry out in frustration for not being able to hold my own children. I had started losing quite a bit of weight and got down to 110 pounds on my 5-foot 9-inch frame due to the inability to keep down solid food. I was suffering heart palpitations regularly and my pulse would race while simply trying to walk across the living room. Finally, in 2012, I visited a doctor who had looked over my past medical history and believed he had some answers for me. As fate would have it, as a Gastroenterologist, he happened to be one of the world's leading specialists in a condition linked to a little-known genetic disorder which produced many of my symptoms. He knew exactly what we were dealing with as soon as I walked in the door.

He referred me to a whole host of new specialists, and I underwent a battery of testing to confirm the diagnosis. Most importantly, I had genetic testing done which focused on connective tissue disorders including Marfan Syndrome, Loey's Dietz, and Ehlers Danlos Syndrome. After three months of waiting for genetic testing to return results, we had both good and bad news. The genetic panel had failed to identify any mutations suspected of causing my symptoms. Testing from the Electro Cardiologist confirmed a diagnosis of Postural Orthostatic Tachycardia Syndrome, or POTS, which was causing my racing heart, dangerously low blood pressure, and near fainting episodes. Further GI testing had confirmed a diagnosis of Mast Cell Activation Disorder, referred to as MCAS, which was causing my weight loss and problems with processing food. Both of these conditions are known comorbidities of a specific genetic connective tissue disorder known as Ehlers Danlos Syndrome. Although I was disappointed that it was a diagnosis of exclusion, we had a name for my condition, and I knew we were finally on the right track.

I do not want to go into every symptom of the disorder, but a basic understanding of the condition is needed to understand what set off the chain of events that led up to the most life altering event I had ever encountered. Ehlers Danlos Syndrome, or EDS, is a connective tissue disorder in which there is a mutation in the genes which code for collagen. Collagen is found in nearly every major body system including your joints, blood vessels, eyes, etc., so when it is faulty, you can have a wide range of symptoms. People with this condition suffer from hypermobility, multiple recurrent joint dislocations, widespread body pain, easy bruising, muscle weakness, and most severely, aneurysms. The effect of faulty collagen on the blood vessels can be deadly and can range from small vessel ruptures to dissections of major arteries. It is a poorly understood condition, and until recently, it was thought to be extremely rare. At the time of my diagnosis, I was thought to have a less deadly form of the disorder, but I was always managed closely by a whole team of specialists including a Cardiologist, a Cardiac Electrophysiologist, a Geneticist, a Neurologist, a Gastroenterologist, and an Internist. Even with the amount of care I was receiving, we never thought I would be much of a risk for the more deadly vascular complications.

With a firm diagnosis and a plan of care for how to treat my disorder, my health slowly began to improve over the next few years. I still had some complications as far as pain and keeping my heart rate under control, but my condition seemed to be much more stable. It was amidst this period of returning to better health that we moved to the farm. At the time, I had high hopes for my continuing future recovery. I had found new specialists in northern Oklahoma that could manage my conditions closer to our new home. With the amount of health monitoring I had, there was nothing about my life at that time which pointed to the fact that I may be in any immediate danger. That all soon changed.

Chapter 2

A Harmony of Despair

"People are scared man, they're scared of the void."
- Joe Rogan

I awakened that fall morning to see John and the kids off to school like I had done so many times before on any given weekday. While going about my morning routine. I noticed a small amount of swelling on the right side of my face near my jaw line. I was not too concerned about it since I thought it was more than likely a minor allergic reaction to something in the environment, so I took a Benadryl and went about taking care of the household duties. Throughout the day, I took a couple of pictures of the swelling and sent them to John to keep him updated on how it was looking as well as the lack of progress it had made. I had no accompanying symptoms such as shortness of breath, tightness in my throat, palpitations, or lightheadedness, which could signal a medical emergency. The swelling was minimal, but persistent so I decided to take a nice hot bath and give the antihistamine more time to kick in. I did not experience any pain in my face or neck, and the whole situation was only a minor inconvenience as far as I was concerned. After bathing, I got dressed before fixing my hair and makeup, and then headed to the living room to relax on the couch and read. I was excited to check the latest news on the presidential election for any early exit polls that may have been released. John and the kids were expected to arrive home within the hour, and I wanted to be ready since we were planning to take the kids with us to the nearest polling center so they could experience the process of voting.

As I was casually scrolling through the news feed on my phone, I suddenly heard what sounded like an explosive gunshot erupt throughout my skull. With no time to react, I immediately got hit with what I can best describe as an avalanche of electricity which originated from the very top of my head and permeated through every inch of my body, before finally terminating at the tips of my toes. As the unpleasant sensation progressed swiftly downward in one single wave, it felt as if the outer layers of my shell were being peeled away from the core of my physical form. Bracing myself for what may come next, I then felt the most unimaginable pain radiating from the base of my head. The pain felt as if I had endured all of the bones and flesh being ripped violently from that area and only a gaping hole had been left in the wake of what had just taken place. The room began spinning and blurring as I centered all my intent on focusing my thoughts.

I cannot put into words the instant panic which hit me. I knew immediately that something severely life altering had just happened, I desperately wanted to escape the situation, but there is nowhere to run when your own body has become your prison. The truth was that I was alone, and I required life saving measures which I knew I could not provide for myself. I fought through the panic and immediately began trying to assess the situation and determine what my chances of survival were. My first thought was that I may have been shot in the head. Living in a flimsy old trailer house, the construction did not offer the sturdiest of walls and it would not be out of the question for a bullet to easily penetrate the thin exterior. Just a few days prior, while checking the fields, we had noticed teams of coyote hunters out with their dogs and hunting rifles scouting the area. Had they returned to the area? A team might have been hunting in the field behind our house and a stray bullet had found its way directly where I was sitting. I focused all my attention on my upper back to see if I could feel the sensation of any blood running down it, but I could not identify any, so I dismissed a gunshot as a possibility. With the obvious eliminated, my next thought was that I had probably ruptured an undiscovered brain aneurysm related to my condition. How could this happen? I had been monitored so closely in the last few years and regularly had scans of my brain performed. Could they really have missed a brain aneurysm? Whatever it was, my heart was breaking because I knew instinctively that the damage had been too catastrophic for me to ever completely recover.

A sense of immense weakness began to overtake my body, and as I felt my life fading away, my thoughts turned to my children. They would be home soon. I became frantic, knowing that they would be the ones finding my lifeless body on the couch when they arrived home from school. How could they ever recover from such a sight? Each day around the time I expected them home, I would sit on the couch facing the front door, waiting for our kids to run in first thing and give me big hugs and kisses before telling me all about their day. I could just imagine their happy little faces as they came running in like they had done so many times before and slowly starting to realize that something was terribly wrong. The thought was too much to bear.

I did not want to become the most terrible thing to ever happen to them. I began desperately begging God to not let them find me because I knew that they would never get over it. Was there any alternative? My thoughts turned to John. I knew his gentle nature and that he would never get past it either. I tried to tell myself that maybe he would have a better chance of working through it, but I knew it was not true. A flood of realization and panic began to wash over me. "Oh God! This is really, really bad. This is happening. I am really dying. This is it." There was no good solution here. Someone had to find my body, and it was going to be someone I loved. There was no way around it. The thought of being separated from the three people in this world who filled my spirit with so much love was unbearable. My heart was breaking so deeply that I could find no words to express the depths of my sorrow. My broken spirit wept with overwhelming grief for so long that I lost all track of time. I found myself in such despair that I had given up any concern for my physical body. The excruciating pain I had initially felt had stopped long ago and I could no longer feel any physical sensations. At some point, I tried to reel in my emotions and decided to look around. It was then that I began noticing where I was.

I was in complete darkness yet could see everything all around me. It was not anything like being in a pitch-black room. I did not feel like I couldn't see because it was dark, I could see everything, but there was just nothing there to see. The darkness went on for what seemed like forever in every direction. I looked down to see if I could see my own hand, but it was shrouded in darkness. Since I could not see it, my next instinct was to try to clap my hands. It was then that I realized that I no longer had any form. Strangely enough, this did not bother me. My existence in that state seemed natural and I accepted my new form without a second thought.

I never lost consciousness during the transition from life to death and I was fully aware of my thoughts the entire time. Being a born again Christian and a Southern Baptist pastor's wife, I was wholeheartedly expecting to be greeted by loved ones and whisked away to a beautiful heavenly abode immediately following my death. "To be absent from the body is to be present with the Lord" they would always say at church. I had no reason to doubt it. I began looking around expectantly for a light to shine down from the darkness and guide me, or a tunnel to appear, or even a familiar face to greet me. We have all seen the death sequence depicted in bad made-for-T.V. movies, and that was basically my expectation. I fully expected one of these scenarios to unfold soon and lead me to eternal bliss.

I prayed while I was there waiting expectantly for someone or something to appear. I wondered if John and the kids had arrived home yet and found me. I prayed that if they had, that they were okay, and that God would protect their minds and send them comfort. I also prayed that they would find healing quickly and that I would be able to be reunited with them one day. Despite my initial reluctance, I had now started to fully accept that my earthly life was over, and I tried to begin preparing myself for what I believed could be the next step.

"Okay, so they were wrong about the tunnel, what comes next? I should probably be standing in front of God at judgment anytime now." I fervently began praying that Christ would stand in my place and that I would be judged based on His righteousness alone. Even though I had been saved and baptized, fear struck me. I wanted to believe that I would easily pass straight into Heaven, but what if I hadn't done enough? I was all too familiar with the depths of my own sin. I knew that I could never make it into Heaven on my own merit. As a child in Sunday School, I was taught that my salvation is not based on works. But when you find yourself at that moment, and you are convinced that you are about to spend an eternity in Heaven or be cast into an eternity of torment, you pray that you are found worthy. So, I prayed, and I waited. And yet, nothing.

The more time that passed, the more I started to realize just how cut off I was from everything. I started to panic. Was this it? The afterlife? It was like no one could or would hear me from the barren chasm where I now found myself captive to the darkness. I could only feel vibrations of a universe teeming with life and creation all around me, but it was all out of my reach. I felt like my essence had been placed in an invisible box and I was not allowed to be a part of everything else in existence. For whatever reason I was isolated, utterly alone, unimportant, and ultimately forgotten. I had just suffered the loss of everyone I loved, and now I found myself separated from all else in creation. I began to sob inconsolably once again, but it did not matter. There was no comfort to be found in this place. Nothing was permitted to distract me from the endless aching I felt in my soul.

There was a rawness to my emotions and I felt as though my consciousness had been fully unboxed for the first time. My being was completely exposed, and the contents of my soul were placed in full view of myself. Every emotion I was feeling was laid bare and amplified by the fact that I, myself had no form and was in all totality just my thoughts and emotions floating in this abyss. My panic only grew as my cries continually went unanswered. I started realizing the gravity of the situation. This was not the heaven that I had learned about my whole life, yet it wasn't hell either. I was lost somewhere in between, void of any love or consolation, with only my thoughts to keep me company.

My mind reeled as I searched desperately for answers. Why didn't I make it to Heaven? Did they find me as unworthy as I had always felt? Why was I never enough? My soul thirsted for love and acceptance from my Creator, but instead I had been thrust into this cold uncaring desert. I started to examine myself more intensely: my thoughts, my beliefs, and my intentions during life. I soon became painfully aware that my soul was consumed with fear. It always had been. My own fears had separated me from experiencing the fullness of love in life and in death. Why had I allowed fear to build a fortress in my heart? In trying to keep out the bad, I had unintentionally locked out everything good with it. If I was currently residing in the emptiness of my fears, then the fullness of love was in the absence of fear.

As I sat and mourned these truths, I began to feel a presence far off to my back left side. It wasn't holy or evil, kindred or foreign. I couldn't even tell if it was human, but his essence was that of a masculine nature. I saw no form, but only sensed him there, a shadow in the darkness. As he approached closer, he sent the impression to my mind that I was only in a holding space, and I would not be there for eternity. The hesitant kindness he showed seemed sterile and gave me the impression that he was breaking the rules by intervening in an attempt to calm the suffering of my spirit. I was thankful for it. For the first time since arriving, I felt a small sense of relief as some of the burden of uncertainty was lifted. At that, I felt a tug and began soaring through the open expanse with the male presence close by for the journey.

Ahead in the distance and off to my right, a faint point of light with a soft purple glow started coming into view. As I drifted closer, it glowed brighter with increasing intensity until it became clear that what I was witnessing was actually a network of pink intersecting lines floating in a giant purple cloud. The thought instinctively came to mind "That is the Fabric of Humanity." It felt like a fundamental truth of existence had been revealed to me by my companion. For those fleeting moments, everything made perfect sense and I saw all life there in perfect harmony and existing as it was always intended to be. It was a stark contrast to the hopeless abyss which I had just left. If darkness had been the manifestation of fear, this place was the physical embodiment of love.

The Fabric of Humanity looked like a scientific map of brain neurons. It was pink in color with spidery appendages branching off each other and linking to one another at converging points. It glowed, sometimes very brightly yellow, at certain junctions where those consciousnesses were joined in emitting such intense love. The immensity of its brilliance radiated throughout the purple nebula cloud which completely encircled the structure. It was a harmony of souls filled with all human knowledge and emotion and I was overwhelmed at its existence. This mysterious eternal source held the unified goodness of mankind spanning through past, present, and future generations, yet existing outside of time as we know it. Its beauty shone through the darkness with the highest importance of all creation, and I wanted so badly to draw closer and join it. Instead, I watched as it shrunk from my view while I continued to sail towards my destination at the hand of the unseen force directing my path.

The next thing I was aware of was awaking with a jolt as my body experienced a hard restart and my mind rebooted back into this reality. My consciousness had remained intact throughout the return transition, but my ability to perceive and experience my current physical surroundings had been restored in that instant. I found myself slumped over on the couch in a strangely contorted manner. I immediately felt the agony of an intense searing pain rushing throughout my head. It was as if hot lava was trying to burn through every vein in my skull. The ringing in my ears caused my hearing to be disorientingly muffled as I heard the television playing in the background but couldn't make out any of what was being said.

I struggled to sit myself up, but I quickly realized that my right arm was no longer functioning properly. I fell back on the couch repeatedly with each failed attempt to sit up as I willed my arm to support my body just enough to propel me toward getting help. Exhausted, I lay there visually searching the room until I was able to locate my cell phone which had dropped from my hand during the last moments of the medical crisis. I wriggled my body over to the opposite end of the couch and was able to reach my phone to call my father-in-law who was working in the field across the street. He answered almost immediately, but when I tried to speak, my words came out unrecognizably garbled. I resorted to repeatedly slurring "911, 911 911", but just the weakened sound of my voice alone had alerted him to the fact that something was terribly wrong. "Mindy, hang on, I'm coming right now." His words were such a relief to me. They meant that I would no longer have to face this alone and that my children would not have to find me this way. As I sat and waited for him to arrive, I knew that I had to have suffered a stroke. My aunt had a massive stroke when I was a teenager and it had left her paralyzed and unable to speak. I was terrified that this could be my destiny too.

My father-in-law arrived within minutes and sat with me until John got home to take me to the hospital. We had a thirty-minute ride down nameless country roads ahead of us before we would reach the small rural community hospital. Due to our extremely remote location, calling an ambulance would have taken longer for emergency services to locate our home than just having John drive me, so we opted for the latter and the men quickly got me loaded into the car. Once on the road, I called the doctor who had diagnosed my genetic disorder to let him know what was happening. He had become almost a friend to our family since we saw him so often to manage my condition. He had previously given us his personal cell phone number to use just in case of something like this and I was so thankful to have his reassuring voice on the other end of the phone during the whole car ride. He was highly concerned as he listened to me slur my words and struggle to form any coherent thoughts as I tried to describe what had just happened. As he spoke to John he pressed, "Get her there, I'm afraid she might be having a massive stroke."

Once we had safely reached the ER, the staff wheeled me back to radiology and ran a couple of different scans of my head. They injected me with dye to get a good look at all the blood vessels, but being a small rural hospital, they were unable to find the source of my symptoms with their limited equipment. My arm had started to regain some movement and my speech was starting to clear over the hours I was there, so the emergency room physician in charge of my care chose not to run any further tests. She had treated me once before and was knowledgeable about my health conditions, but she reluctantly sent me home that day stating that she could not admit me since the tests they had run had not shown anything abnormal. The ultimate response to my condition by the emergency room staff reflected no sense of urgency or concern, and I was sent home with a ridiculous diagnosis suggesting that I had strained a muscle in my neck resulting from the bones shifting. Against our pleas, I was released home with no real diagnosis and no treatment. I was instructed to take Tylenol for pain and follow up with my neurologist. I was also told to return to the hospital if my symptoms returned. Unbeknownst to us at the time, her decision to send me home that day would result in the beginning of years of unending torment in my daily life.

I returned to the ER the next morning after the burning in my skull reached indescribable levels of pain once again. I had become lightheaded and felt myself becoming increasingly confused so I called our church friend Laurie to see if she could come get me. Hearing my voice, she rushed to pick me up and take me back to the same hospital I had visited the day before. We were hopeful that on returning, the doctors would run further tests and would be able to identify what had been missed in the scans the previous day. Instead, we were dumbfounded as I got greeted with disbelief and treated like a hypochondriac or a drug seeker for returning.

Having worked as a nurse, I knew the lingo and the attitude which was being directed towards me. In my weakened state, I begged the staff not to give me any pain medicines, but to instead order different tests that could give a better look at the region where the popping sound had occurred. I knew that they had missed something the previous day and if they did not find it, I would more than likely not survive another episode. This time no imaging was performed, and I was discharged with the suggestion that the symptoms I was experiencing were the result of previously diagnosed migraines. Unbelievably, I was sent home once again with the doctors refusing to acknowledge the gravity of what I had endured, leaving me feeling completely defeated and hopeless.

I sometimes think back to this time and wonder what actions I could have taken to ensure that the medical staff pressed harder to find the true source of my complaints. Was there any way I could have advocated better for myself? The one thing that comes to mind is that despite the obvious physical symptoms which presented that first day, I did not "act" sick. Living with a connective tissue disorder which causes multiple recurrent dislocations of my joints, I had become a master at hiding my pain and acting well despite constantly feeling unwell. I believe this ability to almost completely mask my sickness certainly worked against me in this situation. Outwardly, I was able to speak plainly without yelling and crying while inwardly I was enduring the most tortuous pain I had ever encountered. If I had any responsibility in the failure to properly identify the cause of my sufferings, this most definitely was it.

Returning home that night, Laurie graciously offered to let me stay with her family since they lived in town and much closer to the hospital than we did. With no real answers as to what was causing my sudden symptoms, I was terrified to be home alone and away from immediate help. I was faced with one of the hardest decisions I had ever been presented with in my life. When I got married, I never imagined I would even consider moving out of our family home and away from my husband and kids for any period of time. But when I needed my loved ones more than ever, I chose to pack a small bag of my belongings, hug my children and husband tightly, then walk away from everything I loved to move in with another family. Although my heart was breaking into a thousand pieces, we knew that this was my best chance of survival.

Working with only a diagnosis of migraines, no one understood just how fragile my condition was besides those who had witnessed the change in me firsthand. Once fiercely independent, I now refused to drive because I was scared that I may lose consciousness while on the road and put others in danger. Once known to strictly follow doctor's orders, I now refused to take any medicines because they made my skull burn more intensely. I know that rumors must have been flying while neighbors watched as I moved out of our family home with no real outward reason that could be identified. At the time we needed support the most, there was none to be found. There were no meal trains organized to ensure that my kids were being fed nutritious meals in my absence. There was no extended time off offered to John while he dealt with trying to hold our family together and pay the endless stream of medical bills rolling in. There were no supportive phone calls from church members calling to check in on how the family was holding up during trying times. All the powerful things which people typically draw together to do in a show of support for others going through hardships, were sadly absent from our lives when we needed it the most. Since no one really knew to be concerned, no one really showed any, that is, except for Laurie and her family.

Although we barely knew them at the time, once I moved in with Laurie's family, I ended up staying there for about a month. We soon grew to be very close friends with late night T.V. marathons, game nights, and family dinners together. Laurie would plan out nightly family dinners so that John and the kids could come visit me in the afternoons and we could share a meal together. It never seemed like they lasted long enough. The end of the night goodbyes would be so hard as I put on a brave face and gave the kids hugs and kisses. John and I would linger on the front porch to have a moment of alone time amidst the bizarre circumstances. Although the arrangement was unconventional, I was so grateful for the time we got to spend together.

Laurie's career as the owner of the town's dance studio afforded her the ability to stay home with me during the daytime so I would not have to be alone while I continued to have frightening episodes. Although I never experienced the loud pop again, I was still nearly fainting multiple times a day and I constantly had the excruciating burning pain coursing through my skull. This amazing couple sat by my side each day and talked me through each scary event and their immense kindness was a welcome respite from the physical battle which I was facing at the time.

A few days into my stay with Laurie, John made the difficult decision to sell our home near the family farm to buy one closer to emergency services. He searched earnestly for a house in town and quickly bought one located within blocks of the hospital where I would be close to emergency medical care. I was so happy to finally be back home with my family, but even after a month had passed, part of me was terrified of being alone. I still was not healed from whatever had taken place on the farm that day and the possibility of experiencing it again while alone filled me with fear.

With John and the kids at school during the weekdays, I began sitting with the front door open and 911 pulled up on my phone in case an episode started in which I felt like I was going to lose consciousness. I had mastered holding onto my phone with my finger hovering over the send button so it would directly dial 911 if I lost movement in my arm again. This same routine continued daily for several months.

Over the course of the next few months, I regularly saw my neurologist and he was aware of my ongoing struggles. Unfortunately, he was one of the main forces behind the dismissal I had been receiving from emergency services since they would review my chart and then consult with him. During my initial follow up appointment with this neurologist, he wrote off my complaints of stroke-like symptoms as being a result of hemiplegic migraines, a type of headache which can produce symptoms mimicking a stroke. I was told to find ways to relax and reduce my anxiety during these episodes since they were not dangerous. He also instructed me that I did not need to continue to seek emergency care for them since they were non-life threatening. Trying to follow his professional advice, whenever I would start feeling increasingly strange, I would run a hot bath in order to soak in it to try to relax until the feeling passed. I can remember one time in particular when I had decided to try to shave my legs while soaking and I quickly realized that I did not have enough fine motor control of my right hand to be able to even grip the razor. I could lift my arm part way, but my hand just hung there lifelessly. Knowing that I was having yet another episode, John came into the bathroom to be with me because he knew I was scared. He sat beside the bathtub and stroked my back to try to soothe me as I curled up in the water crying out of pure frustration. This was hell.

Despite what every doctor was telling me, I knew that my body was in a constant state of being near death. It had been over a year since the initial event which began this downward cascade, and I still felt as if I was living with one foot in the world of the living, and one still firmly anchored in the afterlife. Every day was filled with intense, never-ending agony and fear and I sunk into a deep depression as I felt overwhelmingly alone. While the physical suffering was immense, I was equally afraid of returning to the emptiness of the void. It seemed that there was no place between Heaven and Earth which would offer me any rest.

By this time, I still had not told anyone about my experiences on the other side. Although I had full memory of what had transpired over there, I was not yet ready to confront its meaning. I was not sure if I wanted to share what I encountered with anyone. I was very embarrassed by it. How could I ever explain that as a Christian pastor's wife Jesus did not come for me and that I had instead been placed alone in a dark abyss? How could I ever tell them? Who would believe me?

I would call my family members and weep uncontrollably, but they did not know what to think since so many doctors had checked me out and said I was physically okay. While some loved ones began questioning my mental health, I began questioning my ability to withstand much more suffering and became largely apathetic toward life. I became angry with God and wrestled with him constantly. Why had he returned me to this life only to see me live in endless suffering? It was not only taking a toll on me, but it was also breaking my strong husband and causing my children to live in fear. Every day of our lives was filled with uncertainty. Although we had always been an incredibly close family, in my distress I considered moving back in with my mother to ease the burden this was putting on my husband and kids. When I brought it up to John, he opposed it with everything in him, so I stayed, but I knew something had to change.

Chapter 3

Emerging From the Dark

"Hope is being able to see that there is light despite all of the darkness."
- Nobel Peace Prize Winner Desmond Tutu

Determined to begin the process of physical healing despite a lack of diagnosis, I resolved to take charge of my own wellbeing by pursuing those things which I could control. Having never regained my hearing after the initial incident, I decided to first turn my attention to my recent hearing loss. I was struggling to communicate effectively and had been largely relying on lip reading to understand what those around me were saying. We had also started displaying closed captioning on our television so I could follow along without having to turn the volume up to unreasonable levels. Although I knew that I was suffering severe hearing loss, I also had constant deafening ringing in my head which had never stopped. When reporting this to my neurologist, he was indifferent and acted as if I must be exaggerating my condition since the ER scans had not shown anything abnormal. He also refused to do any further testing or send out any referrals since I "looked fine" to him. This only served to confirm what I already knew. If I was ever going to conquer this unexplained condition, then it would be through my own doing.

As a nurse, the last thing I wanted to do was to take my health concerns online to consult "Dr. Google," but in my desperation, that is exactly what I did. Due to the lack of medical care, I had been receiving, I wanted to see if I could find any kind of help for the troubling ringing in my ears. My hearing issues seemed to be the least life-threatening thing I was dealing with and the one issue which possibly had the potential to heal the most quickly. During the course of my internet search, I stumbled upon 432 Hertz music. According to proponents of this form of sound therapy, music tuned to certain specific frequencies can produce beneficial healing effects to the mind and body. I do not know if it was just wishful thinking, but some of the tones seemed to help mute the incessant ringing to some degree. I also very much enjoyed the beautiful tones and the sense of calm the music promoted so I began listening to it each day. I was overcome with awe as the peaceful feeling it evoked was similar to the feeling of serenity that I had felt when in the presence of the Fabric of Humanity.

Given my fundamental Christian beliefs prior to the events of the last year, I would have never considered listening to meditation music as an acceptable practice due to it being related to new age teachings, something I had always been strictly warned against. But in response to my earnest prayers for healing, it seemed that even my God continued to ignore my pleas for help and would offer no comfort. Although I had miraculously returned from the other side, my sense of ultimate abandonment by God did not end after I exited the Void. Not only was I physically broken, but I was also spiritually broken. I was living with first-hand knowledge that there was a Living Force on the other side which permeated everything in existence, but I had to also live with the justified belief that this Living Force had no concern for me. Everything about who I previously was had been painstakingly dismantled at the hand of this Force over the course of the previous months and I was so tired of fighting for any ounce of hope. It was then that I decided to just let go. I quit begging for help. I gave into the fundamental fact that I ultimately had no say over if I lived or died. If I was going to survive this or find any kind of healing, then it was up to the universe to direct my course. I had done all I could.

Miraculously, in the following weeks, I began to notice that my frantic prayers for forgiveness for whatever offense I could have possibly committed to deserve this agony slowly began to turn into deep meditations of self-acceptance and self-love. This state of being was a new experience for me as I was gently guided by my inner spirit to quit speaking and to start listening during my times of divine focus. And as I listened, I started to understand that my experiences of suffering were necessary for my own spiritual growth and wellbeing. I instinctively knew this was a core truth of my own personal journey. Although I had endured so much, I decided to embrace the fear, the torment, and the unknown as an act of perfect love from beyond my own understanding.

A change was seen almost immediately in my life following this essential understanding becoming rooted deep within my soul. A drastic and much welcomed course towards healing and total restoration began. During my daily meditations, I began to feel the presence of blue healing light radiating down all around my head and neck. It created a warm enveloping cloud around me which caused the most painful areas of my body to tingle. This would last about 30 minutes each time it happened, and slowly I began to see slight improvements in the severity of my symptoms. I would tell John excitedly that it felt like the hand of God was holding something together in my neck and was preserving my life. For the first time in a long time, I was starting to have hope! I had total assurance in my soul that recovery was on the horizon and that this was a journey which I was going to survive.

Due to the continuing lack of professional medical care for my ongoing symptoms, our family ended up selling our small-town home and once again moving, this time to Oklahoma City. The larger hospitals in the city provided state-of-the-art equipment and leading specialists in their respective fields. It was here that I finally got the assessment and care that I had so desperately been needing all along. It had been over a year and a half since my incident at the farm and it was well past time to finally get some much-needed answers.

Once we were settled into our new home, we decided to try out a streaming television service instead of connecting to the traditional satellite cable to which we had usually subscribed. Strangely enough, over the course of the first few days with the streaming service, we received a number of commercials for the large hospital system located a few miles down the street. Whether it was an act of demographic profiling, fate, or a combination of the two, what happened next was most certainly beyond the calculated probability of pure chance. Each one of the hospital advertisements highlighted a story about a physician who had saved the life of a patient against all odds. Once an advertisement had started, you could advance past it after thirty seconds had been played, and most of the time this is what we chose to do. But at times, due to whatever reason, we would allow the commercials to play through their full course. During one of these times, I had briefly overheard a young nurse speaking about collapsing in the shower. Since I didn't catch the full story due to being distracted, I wondered what the cause of her collapse had been. I was vigilant to see if I could catch the commercial if by chance it happened to play for us again.

No more than an hour later, the same commercial began playing again. This time I paid close attention, out of medical curiosity more than anything. It may sound somewhat strange, but formerly working as a nurse, I sometimes enjoyed watching medical mysteries and trying to determine the diagnosis before it was revealed. At the time, I had no idea just how much the medical mystery of the nurse in the advertisement would mean in light of my own undiagnosed mystery event. After so much time had passed, I had all but given up on ever finding direct answers since initial scans had ruled out the diagnosis of it being a brain aneurysm. I watched as the nurse in the video described waking up that morning and stepping into the shower. When she leaned back to rinse out her hair, she heard a loud pop in her head. Dropping to the ground, she crawled to help while realizing that she had lost the function of her arm. She contacted her primary doctor, who was featured in the commercial, and was directed to emergency care. There she received a prompt diagnosis and treatment for a rarely seen condition. Her primary care doctor continued to monitor her status after she had been discharged and she was doing well all because of the care she had received.

My jaw was literally on the floor as I turned to John and exclaimed "Whatever happened to her is exactly what happened to me!" This was a life changing commercial, but of course it left out the vital information saying what exactly "it" was. Thankfully, they had stated the patient's name and I was able to look up the full video of her story. Near the end of the video was the first time I had ever heard of this evasive diagnosis. Vertebral Artery Dissection. What the heck was that? Through all my time working in nursing, I had never heard of the condition. I quickly pulled up the term on my phone and was shocked by what I found. On their website, The National Institutes of Health describes the condition:

"Vertebral artery dissection (VAD) is a rare cause of stroke in the general population, but one of the more common causes of stroke in patients younger than 45 years of age. Its signs and symptoms can be vague, making diagnosis difficult. Spontaneous dissections have been reported, but incidental minor trauma typically precipitates this potentially dangerous condition. Patients with connective tissue disorders are also at increased risk. Ehlers-Danlos Syndrome is the most common connective tissue disorder that can cause vertebral artery dissection. (Britt & Agarwal, 2023)"

I could not believe it. There it was in black and white relating directly to my known connective tissue disorder. This had to be it. My heart broke as I continued reading and realized just how lucky I had been to survive:

"For those patients that survive the initial dissection, the prognosis is usually good. Approximately 10% of patients die initially. For patients who do survive the initial acute extracranial dissection, the prognosis is good with complete recovery in nearly 80-90% of patients. However, at least 10% will develop recurrent attacks, a major stroke, or death. Patients who have severe neurological deficits at the time of presentation usually do have a poor prognosis. Follow-up angiographic studies have revealed healing in about 60% of patients.

Patients who develop an intracranial dissection have a poor prognosis. Those who present with altered consciousness and neurological deficits do poorly. Intracranial vertebral dissections are often associated with brainstem infarctions, subarachnoid hemorrhage, and death. (Britt & Agarwal, 2023)"

Even after six years have elapsed, it is difficult to read those statistics knowing the poor condition which I was in when I first presented to that small hospital in northern Oklahoma. My neurological defects were undeniable at the time. It also brings to mind the multiple episodes which I suffered in the following weeks and for which I had been instructed to stop seeking out emergency care. Instead of migraines, had I been having recurrent strokes for which I was instructed to take a hot bath and "relax" until I felt better? We were about to find out.

The next day I reached out to the doctor who had been featured on the commercial as being responsible for diagnosing the nurse's condition. Having just moved into town, I needed to establish a new primary care physician and she happened to be accepting new patients. I signed up through the front desk and got an appointment scheduled for later that week. Arriving at the office I was promptly checked in and led back to the exam room. After introducing myself, I proceeded to break down in a flood of tears as I tried to quickly explain all that I had been through over the nearly two years leading up to that moment. I then shared with the doctor how I saw her on television, and I knew that I had the same thing happen as the nurse. I wish I could accurately convey the look of complete disbelief which flashed across that poor doctor's face as she tried to maintain an admirable level of professionalism. I am lucky that she did not write me off as needing a psychiatric evaluation. Although I knew it was a lot to take in, I also knew that this was my chance to maybe find out the truth behind what happened to me, so I had not held back one iota. Giving me the benefit of the doubt, the doctor sent a referral to the top neurologist in the hospital system and working together, they got me scheduled with an Interventional Neuroradiology specialist to finally fully investigate the cause of my ongoing symptoms.

Within weeks of visiting my new Neurologist, I was sent for an invasive test called a cerebral arteriogram. After being prepped, a catheter was fed from my groin up into my brain and dye was injected into the blood vessels there. I was given some medications to help dull the pain of the procedure but remained awake for the duration of it. I can still remember the Interventional Radiologist rousing me on the table and telling me "We found it!" I just laid there and cried while still in a groggy state. The weight of that statement washed over me, at last, after all the suffering, we had found it.

Once out in the recovery room, the doctor visited with John and I and showed us the pictures he had taken during the procedure. There were two large tears on my right vertebral artery leading up to my brain at the C4/C5 cervical level in my neck. The tears were still not fully healed, and the artery was narrowed and blocked by damaged tissue, allowing only half of the normal amount of blood flow to reach my brain. Along the outer surface of the artery, two pseudoaneurysms had formed. Due to the severity of the tears, had I received appropriate treatment at the time of the dissection I would have had a stent placed to help prevent blood clots and protect the site, but due to the passage of nearly two years, the doctor felt it was now contraindicated. Instead, I was placed on an anticoagulant therapy which I will need to take for the rest of my life.

Hearing this news, I had a rush of opposing emotions. I felt relief that we now had firm answers, but I was angry that my complaints had been previously dismissed. I felt validation for surviving unbelievable duress for so long. More than anything, I was relieved that we now knew how to treat the condition and what my chances of a recurrent attack might look like. Throughout this entire journey, one of the hardest things to cope with was the always present uncertainty of having to live through another major episode which would start another cascade of torturous events which followed. I had lived in a perpetual state of anxiety and fear for two years, and with this new knowledge and the professional reassurance of my specialists, I could begin to put those fears to rest.

After being discharged from the hospital, I found that just a month prior to my own VAD, a story had hit national news of a young model who had suddenly passed away as the result of the same condition. I knew that I was quite lucky to have survived the initial dissection as well as the smaller episodes which plagued me afterwards. In a follow up visit with one of my specialists, we discussed these episodes in more detail and were given confirmation that I had likely suffered a few smaller strokes during the weeks following my VAD. I had been dismissed by the personnel at the first hospital so many times that I had literally resorted to sitting in the bathtub while my husband talked me through multiple strokes. With the help of my new medical team, all my symptoms which were previously minimized and outright ignored were being brought to light and explained with hard science. Now that I had my answers, I could at last lay down that heavy burden. Armed with the knowledge that only a definite diagnosis could afford, it was time to focus on healing my mind, my body, and my spirit.

I was soon referred to a neurological hearing specialist who happened to be one of the only ones in the state that specialized in my type of hearing loss. After an examination including a round of testing, it was revealed that I was severely deaf and had suffered a seventy percent hearing loss in my left ear accompanied by moderate hearing loss in my right ear. Due to the severity of my VAD, the doctor determined that I would not be a good candidate for corrective surgery, and I was sent to the in-house audiologist to be fitted for hearing aids. I never thought I would be so happy to be getting hearing aids before my fortieth birthday, but I knew that they would greatly improve my quality of life. It was suggested that with my level of hearing loss, I would benefit from the use of a new type of hearing aid which featured Bluetooth technology and would allow me to connect phone calls, notifications, music, videos and more from my phone directly into the hearing aid. At the time, this was cutting edge stuff and I felt like the bionic woman once I understood how it all worked. When I arrived for the final fitting, I cried as I heard the world as it truly was. It was then that I realized just how severely my hearing had been damaged. For the last two years I had become quite accustomed to living with muted and muffled voices, and I had mainly relied on lip reading and subtitles to get by. I could hardly wait to get home and hear my children's voices as they now were. I knew they had to have changed so much!

As the days passed, I continued to grow stronger, and my physical health began to stabilize. I had gotten into a routine of using a combination of medical treatments, meditation techniques, exercise, and a form of energy healing found in eastern medicine known as reiki. During the height of my agony, John had learned about reiki and took a few courses to learn how best to utilize it in treating my pain and anxiety. For all my own suffering, one should not overlook the love, strength, and devotion which poured forth from my husband during the darkest of times we had faced. He single-handedly took care of the kids, held down a full-time job, took additional side jobs to pay the growing mountain of medical bills, bought and sold three homes, packed and moved between those homes, and if he found any spare time, he focused it all on healing me. One can easily understand why I had fought so hard to survive my VAD and have more time to spend here on Earth with him. I have no doubt that the steadfast love and kindness that he extended towards me daily served to keep me alive when I could not find it within my own strength to keep fighting.

I knew the heavy toll that this ordeal had taken on my mental wellbeing. Although I strived each day to manage my own mental health, I knew, in all honesty, that I needed the help of a trained professional. I had developed complex Post Traumatic Stress Disorder as a result of the multiple recurring traumas I had experienced over the previous three years. I had become terrified of medical settings to the point where I could not even watch a hospital scene on television. Some of my favorite shows from years past now brought about horrific flashbacks of feeling my life hanging in the balance. Sudden loud bangs such as a bowl dropping, or a door slamming would send me into a panic as I would relive the gunshot sound in my head. Every time I would become convinced that a dissection was happening again. Even though I had made great strides physically, I remained withdrawn from John and the kids as I tried to shield myself from being set off by normal everyday occurrences. I hated the fact that JJ and Aneshka could not just be kids and had to tiptoe around me while in their own home. Because of my mental state, it had become a place of perpetual unrest for them as well.

The first outlet we chose to turn to was the church. I thought that if I could get some spiritual grounding, then it might help me in coping with the mental aspects with which I found myself struggling. I still had not shared my Near-Death Experience with anyone, and despite the pain I felt from the abandonment I encountered on the other side, I desperately wanted to be able to find comfort within our religion once again. We began searching for a church near our home so we could hopefully begin attending regularly.

At first, we tried attending the Southern Baptist Church where I was a member during my youth. For several Sundays we showed up to the later morning service geared towards a more contemporary style since it afforded us a chance to sleep in a bit on the weekends. I quickly discovered that as soon as the worship songs started, I would stand as directed then promptly become lightheaded. At the same time, I would have rapid heart palpitations, my palms would become clammy, and I would get sick to my stomach. My first thought was that it might be due to my still healing body being weak, but that did not make any sense because I was able to do much more strenuous things than just standing up and singing, it had to be something else.

After speaking with John about it, we concluded that it may be a Post-Traumatic Stress Disorder response due to the flashing lights and rock concert-like atmosphere. It made sense. I had always been one to have a bit of social anxiety, so the big crowd combined with the loud banging of the drums was enough overstimulation to send me into an outright panic attack. As a family, we preferred a more subtle and traditional church service, but unfortunately that was hard to find at any church in the city. It seemed that every church that we visited put on a full show at the time of worship, even during advertised "traditional" services. Then there was the issue of doctrine. We tried churches in different denominations hoping to find a church that was a good fit, but I found that I had a hard time sitting in a pew and listening to a man speak about a place he had never been. I had not paid much attention before, but I was starting to realize just how much my spiritual beliefs had been altered. Not only that, but there were major differences that were now emerging in my feelings toward humanity and to life itself, and others were also starting to take notice.

Chapter 4

Life Beyond

"It is never too late to be what you might have been."
- English Novelist George Eliot

One of the things which first alerted me to the changes I had been undergoing was that my personality had become noticeably different from what it had been prior to the VAD. While my family had always remained my foremost priority, being an Okie girl through and through, my biggest interests previously centered around church, politics, and college football. Each morning after taking the kids to school, I would return home to check the headlines for the latest happenings on Capitol Hill. In my free time, I would often find a quiet place to complete a Bible study or listen to a podcast discussing current events or religious topics. John and I used to try to one-up each other by finding the most explosive news stories first so that we could discuss the stories we had found that day as we gathered for dinner. We always had a lively debate trying to sway the other to our own side of the argument. That was not an easy task for me since John had gone to college on a debate scholarship and was very well versed in the craft. Despite his obvious advantage, I refused to lose and would often stand my ground by mustering up every ounce of pure fiery spite that I had within me.

Each year as fall approached, we looked forward to the college football season kicking off although it always fueled one of the biggest divides within our relationship. John had grown up in northern Oklahoma with many of his family and friends attending Oklahoma State University in Stillwater which is home to the OSU Cowboys football team. In direct opposition to them, my family was from Oklahoma City and had always supported the OU Sooners football team from Oklahoma University. College football was such a big part of our lives that we proudly hung our "House Divided" flag displaying the logos for both teams on the flagpole outside of our home in preparation for family and friends arriving for Thanksgiving dinner. Each year, the big rivalry game referred to as Bedlam was scheduled to take place on the Saturday directly following Thanksgiving. Not to miss an opportunity to gather over football, our family permanently moved Thanksgiving dinner from the traditional Thursday and set it to instead take place on the Saturday of Bedlam. It worked well for us as both families excitedly came together to share a meal and cheer on their respective teams. Sometimes there were friendly bets wagered such as the losers having to wear the opposing team's colors the following day. It was always in good fun, and it was something which we always enjoyed as a family.

But despite the happy memories, things had now drastically changed for me. I already knew that my views on religion had been rapidly transformed, but I was not quite ready to confront just how much they had changed, much less try to examine what beliefs had taken their place. As far as football is concerned, it was one of the first things to disappear from my new life. I never really regained any interest in the sport, or any other sport for that matter. At one time I had enjoyed watching Mixed Martial Arts fighting, but now the level of violence was absolutely unbearable for me. How could humans willfully do this to each other? Even watching men smashing into each other during a football game had become jarring and seemed unnecessary. The fact that we once cheered as these young men repeatedly hurled themselves into one another and at times irreparably damaged their bodies for pure entertainment was hard for me to accept.

In addition, politics had now become completely off-putting as I had developed a nauseating disdain for the talking heads which seemed to only stoke divisions and give energy to those things which highlighted the worst in humanity. For the first time since I could remember, the news was no longer exciting to me, it depressed me. Where we once were proud of our political leaders and their accomplishments, their lack of true compassion for others now broke my heart. I found myself repeatedly overwhelmed as the issues which prominently stood out to me now were corruption, intolerance, and at times, even outright hatred which was being displayed by politicians on both sides of the aisle. Sometimes our human species seemed utterly hopeless. How did we ever let it get to this? How had we managed to survive while allowing ourselves to stop caring for one another due to differences in race, sexual orientation, religion, or social status? What makes one person or belief more important than another? Why was the world so full of such deep and unfair suffering? When did we lose sight of the fact that we are all in this together and to care for one another is our greatest purpose?

It was all so very overwhelming. No matter where I went or what I was doing, everything in this world seemed much louder and brighter than it was before. Trying to journey anywhere out in public was a constant task in battling the anxiety produced by any combination of external inputs joining together to result in sensory overload. Even when I was home alone, I tried to find ways to minimize my exposure to lights and sounds. I found myself avoiding tv and modern music altogether. Sitcoms were no longer funny, just annoying, and most anything else worth watching was now too violent for me to enjoy. Even music which I once loved had become too harsh to listen to my sensitive soul. Everything was different. I was different.

Occasionally I would notice that I did not feel like I was living completely back in this reality. The feeling had gotten better as more time had elapsed since my Near-Death Experience, but I still battled the persistent thoughts and feelings fairly regularly. Although my experience on the other side had been terrifying, I no longer felt like this Earth was my true home. I felt like I was a complete stranger here. I knew that there was a much bigger reality on the other side of existence, but I wanted tremendously to be able to enjoy my life here with my family. It is the whole reason why I had fought so hard to return. I knew I needed help working through these things, and I felt that I was finally nearly ready to share the full story of what had taken place after my dying moments.

But would anyone believe me? I had been forced to struggle for so long just to convince anyone that I had suffered from the very real and provable medical catalyst which caused my NDE. Would anyone believe me about my experiences in the afterlife? I knew that it was a risk that I would have to take if I had any chance at moving forward and reclaiming what life I had left. Now that my physical body was beginning to stabilize and continuing to heal, I needed help to confront and work through the symptoms of PTSD which had now become painfully obvious I was battling on an almost constant basis.

To fully understand the effects that can be caused by PTSD, I feel it is important to include a brief overview of the condition at this point. I believe there are some notable overlaps which can be seen between the aftereffects of a Near-Death Experience and the symptoms seen in those suffering from Post-Traumatic Stress

Disorder. (We will take a closer look at these common NDE aftereffects in Chapter 7 of this book, titled Experiencing After Effects.) While PTSD and NDEs should not be viewed as mutually exclusive of each other, it is important to note that each person's experience is different. While one may encounter an occurrence of both as in my case, others may experience an NDE without it resulting in the development of PTSD. The opposite of that scenario is obviously true as well. That is, a person may develop PTSD from any form of traumatic event, and not solely relating to a Near-Death Experience.

The Mayo Clinic Staff defines Post Traumatic Stress Disorder as:

"A mental health condition that is triggered by a terrifying event — either experiencing it or witnessing it. Symptoms may include flashbacks, nightmares and severe anxiety, as well as uncontrollable thoughts about the event.

PTSD symptoms are generally grouped into four types: intrusive memories, avoidance, negative changes in thinking and mood, and changes in physical and emotional reactions. Symptoms can vary over time or vary from person to person. (Mayo Clinic Staff, 2023)"

For two years I had been experiencing symptoms from each of the four categories in relation to both my medical journey as well as my NDE. I was regularly tormented by recurrent flashbacks of each of the traumatic events where I felt as if I was reliving the distressing moments again and again. This was especially true with the initiating moment of my artery dissection. I often endured strange sensations, noises, pops, pains, and pressures inside of my skull as my body continued to react to the damage which had been done to my head and neck in that moment. Each bizarre instance would serve to convince me that another artery was ripping open and in response a flood of panic would overtake me as I braced for another death and possible return to the Void. Although I had trained myself to control many outward signs of fear, internally I was experiencing the most severe emotional duress I had ever encountered.

My symptoms did not end there. As previously discussed, I had become emotionally distant from those who I loved most in this world. Although I had tried to remain optimistic due to the positive direction my life had now begun taking, I was still battling a feeling of hopelessness and thoughts of "What if?" What if this was the best that I could hope for? What if I had only been allowed to return to this Earth for a little while? What if my next death hurts more than the first one did? As much as I wanted to move on, my mind would not allow me to. I was stuck. I wanted to spend every waking moment with John and the kids, but I held back from fully reconnecting with them due to my own fears of dying again. I did not want them to get too attached to me and have to live through the grief I had felt from losing them. In my heart, I knew this thinking was flawed, but my mind was constantly inventing ways to try to control the situation and protect itself from more harm.

I was struggling. I knew that I needed to seek out professional help from a mental health practitioner who could offer resources and techniques to help me work through some of the worst symptoms I had been experiencing. In my need, the universe sent a beautiful soul named Michelle. She happened to work with John at the school during the week, but she was also a state licensed counselor who was in the process of switching professions to focus on her own full-time clinic. John asked her for recommendations of local counselors who could work with an adult experiencing medical PTSD. She asked for more details to better understand the situation and once she fully understood our story, she offered to meet with me once a week free of charge. Additionally, this amazing woman sacrificed her lunch hour every Tuesday to drive to our home and meet with me since I was still fearful of driving on highways.

Each week, she calmly guided me through different techniques I could use to control my anxiety and ground myself when I would feel my mind start racing with panic and fear. She listened patiently as I described my feelings related to what had happened with the dissection and the fallout which had followed in its wake. I chose to only share the medical trauma I had encountered with her at that time. I figured it would be the best thing to focus on since I was not sure how she would react to my memories from the afterlife. I was not even sure she could help me in that department. Who could? But in time, with her direction and encouragement, she helped me face my own mortality. In confronting the damage done by my dissection as well as some of the practitioners within the medical community, I was able to fully embrace the fact that I would, in fact, die again one day. It could be tomorrow, or it could be fifty years from now, but ultimately, I would return to that realm for good and there was an enormous and welcome freedom which came with that acceptance. I could feel some of the burden beginning to lift.

My focus was slowly able to turn away from myself and on to the needs of those around me. Over the months, my mind felt like it was finally catching up to the healing which had been taking place in the rest of my body. As my thinking cleared, I knew that I never wanted others to feel as hopeless and alone as I had felt during the early days of my experience, so I began looking to volunteer my time at different charities. I researched several, but after speaking with each coordinator, none of them really seemed like a good fit. One non-profit that I thought might be a perfect match for me in its mission ended up asking me to volunteer by running a marathon. After multiple strokes and a brain aneurysm, I chuckled at the thought, then politely declined. I knew there had to be a good fit for me somewhere, I just had to find it. Little did I know, the universe already had that covered, and it would show up in one of the most unexpected ways.

As my health continued to improve over the course of two years, it came as a complete shock when, sitting down for dinner one evening, I once again found myself reliving the physical cascade of events I knew all too well as signs of another artery dissection. Thankfully, this time the circumstances surrounding it were much different. John and the kids were home with me and we were close to knowledgeable medical professionals who knew how to handle my condition. It all started when I felt a crushing pain in my left ear, followed by near loss of consciousness and severe tunnel vision. A flood of panic overtook me as John rushed me to the hospital where I was quickly assessed and admitted to the Neuro- ICU Step Down Unit for continued testing and observation. How could this be happening all over again? I was doing so well leading up to it. In this instant, it became clear that I may never be fully healed and that my life continued to hang in the balance. Maybe I was fooling myself all along. I did not know how many more of these episodes my body could withstand.

With that in mind, John and I began having the hard conversations. If I were not to survive all of this, what would I want for our children's future? Where should he hold my funeral and what would it look like? Who would be a strong female influence in my children's lives after my passing? What other family members could we count on to step up and ensure John and the kids were doing okay in the days following? Should John remarry? How would that affect the children? There were so many difficult topics to consider, but we also considered those which brought some hope to the dismal circumstances we once again found ourselves in. What would we like to do in the time we still had together? What wonderful memories could we form with our children right now? We began discussing what we would do if we could rewind time and do it all over. Out of these discussions came some of the most life changing decisions we had ever made. As I found myself once again starting over on my healing journey, my beautiful husband began working to find ways to fill my remaining days with joy.

After all our sci-fi sunglasses had been bought and were securely loaded up with the rest of our luggage, we set out for a 7-hour road trip to New Mexico. It was July and John had decided to surprise me and the kids with a vacation to Roswell to attend the annual festival marking the anniversary of the famous UFO crash. I was ecstatic! I had always wanted to visit the area, but as the years had rolled by, we never made it out that way due to having young children. With my health slowly recovering and almost back to normal, it was time to go out and enjoy life a little bit once again.

Along the way, we stayed a few days in a small mining town called Madrid. We rented an Airbnb there and slept in an original mining shack, then spent some time visiting the shops lining the themed main street. Next, we visited Albuquerque for the 4th of July and watched the fireworks lighting up the night sky from the top floor of our hotel. The next day, we climbed the hills at the Petroglyph National Monument to see the rock carvings and drove to the top of Sandia Peak in the Cibola National Forest to take in the breathtaking views. I was amazed that I was physically able to do all these things, especially climbing the hills of the Petroglyph Monument. With temperatures nearing one hundred degrees that day, I had been nervous about trying to attempt such a feat. Even prior to my VAD, I had struggled with physical exertion in extreme temperatures, but I now surprised myself as I easily spent the day climbing to different petroglyphs to examine. I may have been tired by the end of the day, but I was running on pure adrenaline knowing what the next day had in store.

Arriving in Roswell, we settled into our roadside motel before exploring the downtown area of the city. The festival was in full swing out on the streets as lively visitors donned their best alien fashion and visited with vendors selling an array of space themed goods and souvenirs. Each day, we visited the International UFO Museum and Research Center to attend presentations provided by the top Ufologists in the field including Tom Carey and Donald Schmitt, Kevin Randle, Kathleen Marden, experiencer Travis Walton, Frank Kimbler, and Larry Holcombe. After each lecture, we would visit the common area to see the vendor booths and speak more with each presenter about their research.

At the end of each evening, we would return to our hotel and relax by the pool as we discussed our favorite things we had learned that day. It was always entertaining to hear what topics were of most interest to the kids, and their expanded thoughts on each subject. I loved that they had each grown to share a sense of wonder in the unexplained just as I had experienced as a child. By the end of the week, we were all exhausted, but the trip had been such a welcome and much needed retreat for our whole family after the uncertainty of the last two years. Once the last speaker had completed their presentation, we checked out of the hotel, packed up our belongings, and headed out for the long drive home.

John and I discussed the possibility of becoming involved with our local MUFON chapter as we traveled along the hours of open highway. MUFON, the Mutual UFO Network, is the oldest and largest all volunteer UFO investigative organization in the world. Currently, it boasts a case management system with over 130,000 reported UFO sightings and a worldwide team of fully trained certified field investigators. I pulled up the contact information on my phone and sent off an email to the Oklahoma State Director listed on the website. Unfortunately, she had recently stepped down due to health concerns and the Oklahoma chapter had become defunct. Not to be deterred, I reached out to the National MUFON Chief Field Investigator Doug Wilson. Promptly hearing back from him, we scheduled a phone call to discuss the current state of the Oklahoma chapter and what I could do to help get it back up and running efficiently.

I was monumentally thrilled as I waited for that phone call. I could not believe that someone of his caliber within the organization would actually take the time to call and speak with me. Surpassing all expectations, he proceeded to sit patiently and talk with me for over two hours while answering all of my questions about how the network operated. I did not know what to expect going into that conversation, but I remember hanging up the phone and just letting out a sizable "Wow!" I felt that I had finally found my place! Undoubtedly, I knew this was how I could begin giving back. In many ways I felt I could relate with UFO Contactees. While NDEs, and UFOs may seem to be somewhat different on the surface, experiencers have much in common when trying to explain the unexplainable phenomena which they have encountered. They can often find themselves mocked and ridiculed when trying to discuss their extraordinary encounters, leaving them feeling overwhelmingly alone. Unfortunately, that was a feeling I could completely understand. That day I became a member of

MUFON and within a week I was studying to become a Field Investigator (FI).

Once certified as an FI, I launched a social media page for Oklahoma MUFON and worked to arrange local chapter meetings at our downtown library. I immediately began investigating new cases reported through the database as they were assigned to me. Using the Vallee Classification Scale devised by the famous French Ufologist Jacques Vallee, all cases were automatically categorized according to factors such as how closely the object had approached the witness, if there were lingering physical effects noted, or if there was any type of entity encountered. To begin, I would only be assigned category one cases which denoted a simple flyby sighting until I was able to prove I had become efficient enough in the investigative process to be able to advance to more difficult cases. Category two and category three cases represented those cases which involved the presence of physical evidence and entity or abduction cases. These required a new level of skill sets such as securing an active scene, evidence collection, and conducting in-person witness interviews.

Starting out as a new investigator, I was surprised by how many reports we received here in our state. You never would have known it by conducting an internet search for "Oklahoma UFOs," but people all over were witnessing unidentified aerial phenomena in the airspace over our larger cities and around the rural towns dotting the Oklahoma landscape. With each new report, I began finding that while some could easily be identified as meteors, airplanes, and even simple camera artifacts such as lens flares, many of them would remain unexplained after a thorough investigation. The skies above our great state were absolutely active with the unexplained, and the steady stream of new reports was keeping our small team of investigators rather busy.

But just as our fledgling chapter was beginning to grow, the world came to a complete halt as the Coronavirus pandemic hit the United States. In response, officials held daily news conferences as widespread mask mandates and lockdowns were ordered. UFO case numbers dwindled as the world turned their collective attention to this new deadly virus and the restrictions and shutdowns which resulted from it. Every day there were new reports about the numbers of those infected, maps tracking the spread of the virus, warnings about traveling to the newest identified hotspots, and experts revealing the latest updated death toll numbers. The world watched with nervous anticipation for any kind of breakthrough relating to an effective treatment or cure.

What had initially started as a two-week lockdown to slow the spread of Covid 19, had turned into a much longer waiting game. Many grew fearful as the current stock of food goods began to dwindle from store shelves once most trade and travel was halted. Hospitals were over capacity with those currently infected and their medical personnel were in desperate need of more protective medical gear. Uncertainty and concern for the future were the overarching sentiment of the day as we attempted to steady ourselves amidst the pressure of living through unprecedented times.

The truth was that the world had changed, and with it, so too had things within my own family. With John teaching at the district middle school, he and our kids were now at home all day as they participated in a new distance learning setup devised to minimize the disruption to the classroom curriculum planned for that year. As the weeks passed, it started becoming increasingly clear that this new setup was to become our new normal for the unforeseeable future. Despite the terrible circumstances which forced us into this new unorthodox arrangement, I cannot say that I minded having an extended period of time to take a deep breath and regroup from the chaos we had survived over the last few years. While outside our door a pandemic was raging, the time it afforded us to spend together provided the balm of raw conversations enabling deep healing that was desperately needed by every member of our family.

It was amidst this setting that the long-hidden truth of my Near-Death Experience finally came bursting forth out into the open. It had been a somewhat normal day as John was in the kitchen preparing some sandwiches for lunch while we discussed different churches that we may want to try visiting in the future. Like most, he had chosen to handle the stress of the pandemic by turning to a God who could offer him comfort and help ease his fears. But with fear now surrounding us from every side and the uncertainty of death facing us once again, the topic of trying to find a place to worship a God who I knew had cast me aside in my deepest need was all too much for me. I could not hold it in anymore.

I felt the emotions well up inside of me as a dam of pent-up heartbreak and terror was finally released in one explosive moment. All that I had previously fought so intensely to hide revealed itself through a flood of panicked tears. "I died that day, and I did not go to Heaven." My husband and children sat in quiet astonishment as I frantically shared the entirety of what I had endured during my journey into the afterlife. I could see the empathetic anguish set in across my husband's face as he searched his mind for any answers as to why this could have happened to me. In this moment, he understood why I had sat up some nights crying inconsolably for hours without being able to voice what was troubling me so deeply. Although we had previously disregarded stories of Near-Death Experiences as possibly being fabrications or tricks of a dying mind, we now knew the truth was something very different. These experiences were real.

Finally sharing the reality of what had transpired during my NDE with my family was one of the hardest yet most important conversations I believe I had ever had. With John having previously occupied the pulpit as a pastor, I knew what believing my account would mean for those of faith closest to me. I had already battled with the apparent contradictions between my experience and my faith for the last two years and now I was asking my family to help me find understanding where on my own I could find none. Trying as I might to reconcile the differences, I knew that my encounter was contrary to almost every Christian teaching I had learned about the subject of life after death. But despite that, I continued to fight through the shame that I felt as a result of not going to Heaven. For me, this was one of the most emotionally overwhelming and distressing aspects of what I had endured. Not knowing where to turn, we now found ourselves seeking answers from some of the very communities we had once dismissed.

John began diving into research on Near-Death Experiences almost immediately while I decided to wait. I felt it was important to get my experience recorded on paper in its entirety before allowing myself to read any studies about NDEs or the reported accounts of others. I did this to try to avoid any minor influence they may have had on the reporting of my own encounter. As I worked my way through recording every detail of my NDE, I felt the weight of my sorrows beginning to lift as I knew I no longer had to hide the truth, no matter how painful it may have been. It was scary and liberating all at the same time. What followed was a time of accelerated personal growth as I let go of any preconceived notions I had once held and chose to explore what this new reality could afford. It was time to find out why I was returned to this world and what my place was within it.

Chapter 5

Finding Omega

"The true knowledge is not in the things, but in the connections between the things."

- Oklahoma Author Daniel H. Wilson

While delving into my search for a better understanding of the Near-Death phenomenon, I simultaneously focused my time and energy into gathering more knowledge about the history of UFO encounters. About this time, the terminology started to change from the historic, UFO abbreviation which stood for Unidentified Flying Objects, and we started hearing talk of UAPs, or Unidentified Aerial Phenomena. This happened largely in response to the government acknowledgement of videos showing an unknown Tic-Tac shaped object being pursued by a U.S. Naval fighter jet from the nuclear aircraft carrier, the USS Nimitz. This announcement was welcome news for myself, and it offered a welcome distraction from my health concerns and the heavy topic of NDEs. I found that I often needed to take breaks to process some of the intense material found while reading about NDEs, and the UFO subject offered a nice mental break for me since I was not as emotionally connected to the subject matter. Although I was eager to learn more general information about NDEs, I knew that I was not yet ready to confront the deeper implications of my own encounter.

Strangely enough, I often struggled when reading about the wonderful homecoming type greetings that others had experienced while on the other side. When compared to what I had endured, I found that their stories brought back the same overwhelming feelings of inadequacy I had felt during my time in the Void. Why had almost every other Near-Death Experiencer reported going to a Heaven where they were surrounded by loved ones, while I had been cast into utter darkness? As I would try to put the troubling questions out of my mind, I would find myself once again focusing on the UFO phenomenon to distract me. It was a careful balance in which I found myself teetering for several months as I worked to grow my knowledge in both subjects at a comprehensible rate. I was consumed with trying to answer two of the biggest questions we have as a species: Are we alone? And what happens after we die?

Since most of my study was focused on the UFO side of things during this time, my attention quickly got directed towards a technique known as CE5. I wondered if I would have an edge in using this technique given my previous experiences with the unknown dating all the way back to childhood. At the very least, it was worth trying so that I could better understand some of the sightings reported in my MUFON cases. CE5 is an abbreviation for Close Encounters of the Fifth Kind, and it can sometimes also be referred to as HICE, or a Human Initiated Contact Event. Practitioners of CE5 choose to get into a meditative state prior to attempting contact, and some choose to incorporate certain tones which they aim at the sky to help facilitate an encounter. After speaking with multiple UFO witnesses and researchers, I decided to try the technique to see if I could personally get an otherworldly response.

Being a novice at the practice, I was not expecting too much to happen since I had not been a UFO experiencer to date. And while I remained hopeful of a response, I also wanted to use the time to try out our new binoculars and get a feel for their mechanics. The whole family; John, the kids, and I, all gathered out in our front yard on that warm spring night in May of 2020. Our daughter had a neighbor friend staying over for a sleepover at our house, so the girls chose to lay out on a lawn blanket while the rest of us reclined in folding chairs to get an open view of the night sky. It was a beautiful clear night, so it was nice to just be outside together enjoying the crisp evening air.

As John was adjusting the focus on the binoculars so that the girls could get a close-up view of the moon in its waxing gibbous stage, our son J.J. and I sat side by side in our chairs comparing different star maps and compass applications on our phones. Once we had at last turned our full attention to the expanse of stars above us, I quietly closed my eyes and focused my attention on sending goodwill and guiding thoughts towards the cosmos. Somewhat embarrassed, I did not want to draw attention to myself, so I did not alert anyone to what I was attempting. No more than ten minutes had passed before we all saw it. What it was, I am still quite unsure, but whatever it was, it showed up in a beautifully dazzling display witnessed by all in attendance.

At first, there was one quick burst of bright white light, followed quickly by a second white flash just as brilliant as the first. JJ and I gasped in unison. "Did you just see that?" I excitedly inquired. I turned to glance at my son only to see him shaking his head affirmatively in astonishment. Knowing that I would later want to check for any known explanation for what we had just seen, I quickly jumped into investigation mode by noting the time, height, and direction where the lights had been seen. Both bursts of light occurred at 11:11 PM at around a 30-degree elevation, and shone brightly at an approximate stellar magnitude of -3. Each flashed only once, lasting only a fraction of a second and had no trail or forward motion in any direction that we could discern. I noted their position in the sky by recording each to have an azimuth of 318° and 329° respectively. As we sat and discussed what we had just witnessed, another flash bulb erupted just two minutes later in the north-northeastern sky at a 40° azimuth and a 60° elevation. This was followed by another bright burst approximately two minutes later in the northern sky, and one final flash of light two minutes after that, all ending at 11:17 PM. Five singular bright white flashes were seen spanning across the sky over the course of 6 minutes, witnessed by all five of us that night. I began checking my phone applications for any logical explanation for what we had just witnessed.

The Aquarids were active during this time, but they did not line up with the objects we witnessed since their radiant was well below the eastern horizon and had been originating from the wrong direction. There was no way that these flashes could be related to the meteor shower. We also found no debris reentries noted for that night, and the perceived lower altitude of the objects immediately ruled out any satellites, although when checked, none were found which matched what we had just observed. I was simply dumbfounded. As we remained outside for a bit longer, we watched for any further activity while pointing out constellations, tracking satellites, and taking photos of the Moon. After a couple of hours, we decided to turn in for the night and head inside, but we never saw any more flashes of light like what we had witnessed at the beginning of that evening. It was a breathtaking display which I am thankful for and will always remember, but I secretly wondered if it had all just been a coincidence. Had I really been able to make contact with a form of this phenomenon so easily? If so, why have we not seen others doing this more often? I knew this was something that I would need to keep in mind going forward when conducting future investigations.

Only a few weeks later, I found myself attending a sky watch which I had arranged to meet up with a gentleman from one of my former MUFON cases. He and I had stayed in touch after the completion of his case, and he regularly shared new photos and videos with me that he had happened to capture of unknown craft or unexplained lights in the sky. At past events, he had been known to have the ability to call down UFOs and had indeed produced several interesting pictures of unidentified craft to back up his claims. With the winter weather now clearing and affording an outdoor gathering, we decided to finally meet up to see if anything would materialize.

The night we chose for the sky watch was clear and afforded great visibility when we all gathered up on a hill located in what was once part of the old Osage Nation Reservation land. The hill was rocky with wild sagebrush growing in patches around large collections of boulders. Nearby city lights combined with the brightness of the half-moon to illuminate the area well enough for us to see our footing as we ascended the small mound. Once atop, the vantage point gave us a perfect view of the city as well as the surrounding areas below including the nearby airports and a clear sight of the flight patterns of planes taking off and landing.

There were a handful of us in attendance for the duration of the sky watch, with a few others coming and going throughout the night. Those who were in continuous attendance were me, the witness, his colleague, and two MUFON members; one of which is also an experiencer, and the other who opted to stay with the car at the bottom of the hill due to the strenuous trek required. After several hours of viewing the sky, we saw three questionable lights which were not easily identifiable as known commercial craft. Not a bad evening, but honestly, nothing quite mind blowing either. All the lights we had seen had been far in the distance and could have easily been military craft that were not transponding or even drones displaying aviation beacons.

Since it was nearing midnight, we decided to start shutting the sky watch down and began packing up our gear in preparation for the downhill hike which lay ahead. As each of us was getting equipment torn down and packed away, our conversation briefly turned to the suspected correlation between UFO sightings and birds. It was a phenomenon which both of the experiencers in attendance had encountered numerous times before. I listened as they each swapped stories about redbirds, owls, cranes, and black birds, all seen in the presence of other unexplained phenomena or around the time of contact. Some believe these birds are messengers or could even be manipulated screen memories, but one thing was certain for the two experiencers in attendance that night, birds were a recurring theme known to those who have had UFO encounters.

As we stood at the precipice of our descent and wrapped up our enthralling conversation, we prepared our packs for the long downward trek. Just as we had all turned to head down the hill, a large sandhill crane appeared, seemingly from nowhere, directly at the level of a nearby power pole. The wooden pole had lines coming off it at approximately fifteen feet above ground level and we stood about twenty feet away from where the pole itself was planted firmly in the soil. When we noticed the bird, it was already nearly directly overhead. It gracefully flew between the powerlines before swooping down to ten feet over our heads, and then lifting off in an easterly direction. As it passed over, we could easily see the fine details of the bird. White and tan feathers were interspersed and covered the thick body. Individual feathers could easily be seen along the tips of its wings, which boasted a wingspan of close to seven feet wide. It carried its neck in a folded fashion and its two thin legs hung down straight below its body as it flapped its wings and soared up close to eighty feet into the open night sky. All of us stood reticently and watched as it reached the height of its aerial climb and in a quite spectacular display, simply blinked out of existence. There was a palpable and collective gasp of awe as each in our group struggled to make any sense of the unbelievable spectacle we had just witnessed. We waited in silence for several more moments in expectant anticipation of a reemergence, but the creature never returned.

I believe that this event will forever stay at the forefront of my memory as one of the more extraordinary encounters that I have had the privilege to experience. The implications of a seemingly flesh and blood creature instantly ceasing to visibly exist in our reality are quite profound, yet this ability seems to be standard when compared with the manifestations of other unexplained phenomena. Prior to this experience, I had known that spirit beings could materialize and dematerialize in our earthly realm with relative ease, but this was the first time I had witnessed a solid lifeform show this same ability.

I wondered if these different types of entities had utilized similar pathways to enter and exit our reality within an instant. If so, could this pathway be the same one which I took during my NDE? My investigations into sightings of UFOs had pointed to them seemingly being able to instantly manifest physically, while inversely having the ability to disappear in the blink of an eye. The more I was learning about the UFO phenomenon, the more I was beginning to wonder if it had much more in common with Near-Death Experiences than I had initially realized.

I was beginning to understand that there had to be a much larger connection between these two distinct types of experiences, and I was determined to find out what it was. It seemed that everywhere I turned, I was noticing more evidence to support the idea that these two could be part of a unified phenomenon in some way. Books, expert interviews, MUFON witnesses, and my own unexplained experiences were all pointing to this idea that there could be some kind of unknown correlation between NDE and UFO occurrences which warranted a deeper exploration of their collective meaning. I was aware of an effect known as the Baader–Meinhof frequency illusion wherein a person who has taken note of a particular thing will see it repeated with more frequency after taking note of it for the first time. I was sure to keep this effect in mind as the evidence to support a unified phenomenon began to turn up in more and more unexpected places. The last thing I wanted to do was try to force a connection where there was none to be found.

One of the things I did after I had begun strongly considering this correlation was to start incorporating questions relating to Near-Death Experiences into my investigations with Category Three witnesses who had reported a contact or abduction experience. After interviewing the reporting party about their previous contact encounters, I would then ask if they had ever had a Near-Death Experience sometime in the past which they could recall. I was stunned as time and time again these UFO witnesses easily recounted their own temporary deaths and the resulting experiences they had faced while on the other side.

One experiencer had reported multiple recent UFO encounters and had a notable increase in her experiences following an electrocution event which had resulted in her temporary death. Another contactee reported that he had begun having close encounters following a rollover accident on an all-terrain vehicle in which he was crushed and broke his neck. He vividly remembered his Near-Death Experience and could recall all his time briefly passing through a dark abyss. One of the more profound abduction cases I have worked to date featured a young woman who had taken her own life, only to find herself returned to this earth. Shortly thereafter, she endured a prolonged UFO contact event which resulted in a complete change in her life. After the NDE and UFO encounters, she reported that she felt she was now a different person than who she had been before, and that her life was now better in every way possible.

With each newly reported encounter, I would search my mind to try to understand why this overlap seemed to be happening. Could it be the result of a certain type of person being prone to mystical thinking, or possibly due to them having strong beliefs about the paranormal which predisposed them to perceiving these types of events? If so, what would that say about me? I had been very immersed into Christian culture prior to my NDE and had taken a step back from it due to my encounter, but the opposite could also be seen in many who had similar experiences wherein they found religion because of what they had faced. I also wondered if the same effect had been seen from the other side of things. That is, were those in the NDE community also reporting unexplained encounters following their Near-Death Experiences? To find out, I knew that it would mean fully confronting my own encounter, something which I was still unprepared to do. Instead, I chose to turn my full attention to the UFO phenomenon in an attempt to ignore my intensifying NDE questions. But, as life so often does, those issues would come bubbling back up to the surface in unexpected places until they were confronted and fully realized as had always been intended.

Thinking myself clever, I had settled on reading through Whitley Strieber's "*Communion*" during my free time believing that this book would be a straightforward UFO abduction book and would help clear my mind. It was the first book I had decided to read after becoming a Field Investigator for MUFON. Relying on its fame and rank as a New York Times Bestseller, I knew it would be a great place to continue building my knowledge about the alien abduction phenomenon and focus my attention on my passion for Ufology.

It was with this mindset that I began reading through Strieber's book. In it, he details the unexplained encounters which took place at his family vacation home in upstate New York and the resulting journey which unfolded as he searched the deepest reaches of his mind to unravel what had truly transpired during those strange nights. Working with renowned Ufologist Budd Hopkins, Strieber underwent hypnotic regression to recover repressed memories surrounding the missing time he had experienced during his encounters. After one of these intense sessions, Whitley describes an episode in which he returns home restless from the visions that had flooded his memory. After a walk around town to collect his thoughts, he retreats to his home office where he sits alone on the floor. He describes what took place next:

> "As soon as I relaxed, it was as if I had opened the hatch into another world. They swarmed at me, climbing up out of my unconscious, grasping at me. This was not memory, it only worked through a medium of memory. It was meeting me on every level, caressing me as well as capturing me. This emergence was like a kind of internal birth, but what was being born was no bubbling infant. What came out into my conscious mind was a living, aware force. And I had a relationship with it – not a fluttering new one, but something

rich and mature that ranged across the whole scale of emotions and included all of my time. I had to face it: Whatever this was, it had been involved with me for years. I really squirmed.

What might be hidden in the dark part of my mind? I thought then that I was dancing on the thinnest edge of my soul. Below me were vast spaces, totally unknown. Not Psychiatry, not religion, not biology could penetrate that deep. None of them had any real idea of what lives within. They only knew what little it had chosen to reveal of itself.

Were human beings what we seem to be? Or did we have another purpose in another world? Perhaps our life here on Earth was a mere drift of shadow, incidental to our real truth. Maybe this was quite literally a stage, and we were blind actors. (Streiber, 1987, p. 95)"

I was shocked! Here I was once again face to face with an otherworldly encounter which undeniably resembled my own NDE. How did this man's words so closely reflect my same inner thoughts following my Near-Death Experience? In pure disbelief, my first instinct was to dismiss the similarities that I had noticed between Strieber's encounter and my own as merely a stunning coincidence. "It just cannot be," I thought to myself. I read through the passage again, my mind racing. I knew what he was speaking about and that my experience in the Void had interacted in much the same manner. I had been met there by an ancient force which connected with me directly through the vehicle of my own consciousness. This force had also known me intimately throughout my entire existence and understood my every thought. How could this be? This was a whole new aspect of the phenomenon which I had not previously considered. Could the location of my encounter be the "real truth" to which Strieber had been referring? Was it possible that this man was describing an encounter with the same phenomenon I had experienced during my NDE, only he was speaking of the occurrence as it was experienced on this side of the veil?

I had so many questions churning through my mind. There it was, so plainly laid out before me and I knew that I could no longer deny it. More, deeper questions came flooding into my mind. Why was I able to make contact so easily during my first CE5 attempt? Why was I granted the ability to witness the crane disappear in an instant? Why had so many of my UFO contactee cases reported having previous Near-Death Experiences? The evidence was now undeniable for me.

I figured if this connection was indeed real and not some trick of my mind trying to find comfort in connecting, then there had to be others who had noticed this same association in the past. I began an earnest search to find any studies which had been conducted on the subject. To my delight, I came upon an entire book on the subject from the early 1990s written by Dr. Kenneth Ring titled, *The Omega Project*. At the time of its publishing, Dr. Ring was already one of the world's top authorities on Near-Death Experiences having co-founded the International Association for Near-Death Studies (IANDS) with fellow researchers including John Audette, Dr. Raymond Moody, and Dr. Bruce Greyson. Most persons with even a glancing interest in the subject will recognize each of those names as giants of the NDE industry, as they were the first to put their reputations on the line in search of answers to the question, "What happens after we die?"

As professor of psychology at the University of Connecticut, Ring had undertaken previous studies related to NDEs and had published two books related to his findings. The first, *Life At Death: A Scientific Investigation of the Near-Death Experience*, was published in 1980 and focused on 120 reports from NDErs and the similarities which he was able to identify between their accounts. In his second book published in 1984, *Heading Toward Omega: In Search of the Meaning of the Near-Death Experience*, Dr. Ring examined how these encounters served to change the lives of those who experienced them.

Building on the knowledge gathered from his previous investigations into the NDE subject, Dr. Ring next turned his attention to the UFO phenomenon. Incredibly, in a progression of events similar to my own path, he had been given a copy of Whitley Streiber's *Communion* by a colleague who urged him to read it with an open mind while considering how it may relate to his previous study of NDEs. While reading through the book, he began to see why his colleague had suggested the connection, and he quickly set out to begin a new comprehensive study researching the relationship between the two phenomena.

While I do not want to give a full book report covering *The Omega Project*, it is important for our purposes to highlight some of the major findings and conclusions of Dr. Ring's study as they relate to my personal experiences. It is highly recommended that readers interested in further understanding the correlation between UFOs and NDEs from a collegiate perspective purchase a copy of Dr. Ring's book to read in its entirety. It provides the full original battery with compiled responses from the study participants, as well as Dr. Ring's opinions regarding the meaning behind his findings which include a possible human evolution representing a new Omega Prototype.

On the subject of Near-Death Experiencers, previous studies carried out by Dr. Ring during the 1980s ruled out any correlation between demographics including age, sex, race, socioeconomic status, and education with NDE status. In contradiction to those findings, a 2006 study of UFO Abduction Experiencers carried out by Stephanie

Kelley-Romano of Bates College and reported in the Journal of UFO Studies identified a certain prominent demographic in those reporting UFO abduction encounters. Of the 130 participants, there was a higher incidence of women represented with 53.8% reporting as female. Respondents to the study were predominantly white with 85.4% identifying as Caucasian. Percentages of those attending higher education were found to be elevated in the abduction group compared to the general population, signaling that abductees tend to be more highly educated. Of the abductee group, 49.2% reported that they had attended at least some college and 15.4% reported that they had graduated, with 8.7% earning a graduate degree. Marital Status was not found to be a relating factor as approximately half (48.1%) of respondents reported being married, and in the final category, no correlation was found in occupation types reported by the respondents.

Two of the main points which emerged from the NDE/UFO study carried out by Dr. Ring was the discovery of a type of encounter prone personality which was found to be present prior to these transformative encounters, and a collection of aftereffects which were commonly reported amongst both UFO and Near-Death Experiencers following these events. Regarding encounter-proneness, he shares a developmental theory of propensities for extraordinary encounters following his assessment of questionnaire responses to the psychological inventory section of the Omega Project battery.

"We have now in effect set the developmental stage for an extraordinary encounter - either an NDE or a UFOE (experiencer). To summarize our theory to this point, we have a prototype and individual who, coming from a history of childhood abuse and trauma, has developed dissociative tendencies as well as a capacity to become deeply absorbed in alternate realities. Indeed, we can assume that such an individual, by virtue of this kind of psychological conditioning, is well accustomed to such unusual states of consciousness since he has often had recourse to enter them.

What I am suggesting, then, is that these individuals are what we might call psychological sensitives with low stress threshold, and that it is their traumatic childhoods that have helped to make them so. From my own personal point of view, however, these UFOErs and NDErs are actually the unwitting beneficiaries of a kind of compensatory gift in return for the wounds they have incurred while growing up. That is, through the exigencies of their difficult and in some cases even tormented childhoods, they also come to develop an *extended range of human perception beyond normally recognized limits.* Thus, they may experience directly what the rest of us with unexceptional childhood may only wonder at. (Ring, 1992, p. 146)"

Following up on that point, I feel that it is imperative to note that Dr. Ring further clarified his belief that there were doubtlessly multiple other routes which could lead to a propensity for encounter proneness which were not investigated in the study. Other suggested courses in which a person could develop the abilities to access alternate realities include acquiring them during childhood through encouragement of imaginative exploration by parental figures, and through the nurturing of such naturally inborn abilities of the psychologically sensitive child. In a separate inventory, it was further noted that childhood stress related to serious illness also resulted in experiential adults. Regardless of the originating cause in each case, these abilities were found to lead to dissociative tendencies as well as something Ring referred to as psychological absorption. This he defined as "The ability to concentrate and focus one's attention on the figures and features of one's inner reality to the exclusion of events taking place in the external environment." The pairing of abilities to access alternate realities and to register the encounters there is the critical aspect identified in this portion of the study.

Also examined were the key changes most commonly reported following these two distinct types of extraordinary encounters. Statistically significant were the reported psychophysical changes which included increased generalized sensitivities, electrical sensitivities, decreases in body temperature and blood pressure, and experiential reports of noted alterations in nervous system and brain function. Respondents also reported a remarkable shift in their values and belief systems including increases in spirituality, self-love, altruism, and concern for others. Overall, experiencers in both categories reported positive fundamental changes resulting in a sense of universal love and a need to tell others about their encounters.

Dr. Ring's Omega Project remains one of the most important studies to be carried out on the correlations that may be found between the two phenomena. His focused efforts set a new standard in the field of UFO and NDE research and created a basic understanding of how these separate kinds of phenomena can arise in persons who present with a certain type of personality while resulting in similar favorable changes in the experiencer. Years later, the research into the relationship between the two experiences continues. In her 2019 book, *Extraterrestrial Contact: What to Do When You've Been Abducted,* Kathleen Marden shares statistics from ongoing research conducted by MUFON's Experiencer Resource Team which she founded in 2011. She writes:

"I believe it is important to note that MUFON discovered an increased level of Near-Death Experiences on the Experiencer Survey. Among MUFON's three groups, 44 percent of the survey takers stated they'd had a Near-Death Experience. In the abductee group, the level increased to 55 percent, whereas in the contactee group, the level decreased to 35 percent. These findings are consistent with the Omega Project studies that noted psychic awareness, altruistic feelings, and increased spirituality among NDE and UFO experiencers. (p. 123)"

This data brings a new dimension to the Omega Project findings in that it highlights an increased incidence of Near-Death Experiences in the population of those reporting abduction events. According to research conducted by NDE expert Dr. Bruce Greyson, only around 5% of the population has had a Near-Death Experience. It is an incredible finding then that over half of experiencers reporting abduction encounters to MUFON also report having had a Near-Death Experience sometime in their past. It is unknown whether this finding points to a new, yet undiscovered connection between the two, or if it could be related to the underlying encounter prone personality identified by Dr. Ring. Future areas of research may seek to focus on the patterning of these types of encounters in an experiencer's life to determine if their NDE bore any difference on the timing or emergence of UFO contact experiences. Acquiring a better understanding of the way in which these phenomena manifest in an experiencer's life may give way to deeper understanding of their origin and capabilities. In the following chapters, we will examine my own lifetime of encounters leading up to my NDE, followed by the immense and sometimes painful aftereffects I encountered as a result of my journey to the other side. It is my hope that by revealing these sometimes-hidden truths that the reader will gain a more complete knowledge of the ongoing nature of these phenomena in the life of an experiencer.

Chapter 6

Encounter Prone

"Every moment of searching is a moment of encounter."
- Brazilian Novelist Paulo Coelho

Turning my attention to the Encounter Prone Personality as outlined in the Omega Project, it was clear that I had experienced many of the identified traits starting at an early age. On the matter of fantasy-proneness, I had already known that I was not someone who was much for living in the world of fantasy, as my mind was one which had always tended to stick strictly to the facts. As a child, I struggled to make up elaborate stories for school assignments, and as an adult with children of my own, I left the bedtime storytelling to John while I chose instead to sing a goodnight song with the kids. The few times I did try to make up bedtime stories for them, I always just ended up telling them about the mundane things that had happened in the lives of "Cindy and Juan."

During my childhood, I was drawn to the wonderful freedom I felt while exploring the surrounding neighborhoods on my bicycle. I enjoyed inspecting abandoned buildings and creating my own science experiments out of things I would find in nature. Much to my older sister's dismay, I was not a little girl who was interested in playing with dolls or playing school together. Instead, I was always driven by a deep inner yearning to spend my time learning about life and understanding the mysteries of the world. Oftentimes, my sister and I would ride our bicycles down to the Book Mobile together where she would gather as many books on cats as she could carry, and I would fill the basket on my handlebars with anything I could find relating to wonders and mysteries. My indoor playtime normally consisted of working complex puzzles or playing games that involved some type of strategy. Although I always felt a bit different, my childhood was fairly normal in most senses for a young girl growing up in a single parent, lower middle-class household.

In addressing the childhood trauma aspect of the encounter prone personality, I would just like to say that I had my share of traumatic experiences during my formative years. While these events no doubt helped shape who I am today, I cannot fully say that they are the singular cause of my susceptibility to dissociate and enter into altered states of consciousness. For me, I feel there were a couple of contributing factors which led to the development of this ability. Foremost of those factors is the unrelenting pain I suffer because of my genetic connective tissue disorder which went unacknowledged, undiagnosed, and untreated until adulthood.

Having been born with the condition, I have suffered from chronic pain and dislocations from as far back as I can remember. Since we were not aware of the disorder, I was often instructed to "Suck it up" by tending adults and one of the ways I learned to do that was through teaching myself to dissociate at a young age. Reaching upper elementary age, I had realized that I had gained a strange ability to enter into other states which allowed me to block out the pain I was experiencing. I would often go outside on the porch at my grandma's house during the summer and practice this ability, at times speaking with nature, God, or the gentle spirits I felt surrounding me. This inner world became a safe space where I could retreat, heal, and explore other states of consciousness. Oftentimes, I would instinctively ascend to a realm of healing and mentally bathe my small body in radiant white light in an attempt to reduce the overwhelming pain I felt. Although I did not know a name for what I was experiencing at the time, what I was developing during my youth were three of the main characteristics identified as fundamental contributors to the encounter prone personality which include; susceptibility to altered states of consciousness, proneness to dissociative states, and a tendency towards psychological absorption.

While I actively worked countless hours during childhood to develop the previously mentioned coping mechanisms, the final trait identified by Ring seemed to be one which I was unquestionably born with. As early as my toddler years, it was clear that I was a child who possessed some form of psychic inclination. What may be viewed as extraordinary events by others seemed to be part of my natural world growing up. It took me years to finally grasp the idea that not everyone continually has these types of encounters. Here, I will give a sample of the kinds of experiences which were so common in my life during childhood and leading up to my NDE. As you read through, please be aware that like many other Near-Death Experiencers, I see the experiences and life presented in this chapter very much as a "before" version of myself. While these encounters set the stage for who I am today, they do not necessarily reflect my current thoughts and understanding of the phenomena.

My first clear memory of communicating across the veil was in 1984. I was just five years old at the time and we were living in a small rental home on the north side of the city. There weren't enough bedrooms in the house, so my sister and I slept in a set of bunk beds in my mother's room. Since my sister was four years older than me, she got the first choice of claiming the top bunk, and I was stuck with the bottom. It never really mattered much though, most nights I would just end up crawling in bed with my mom. Like most young children, I felt warm and safe there and I preferred sleeping next to her over sleeping alone.

During that time, my maternal grandfather had started to fall very ill with complications of diabetes. Our family could only watch as he lost his leg to gangrene, suffered a series of crippling strokes, and became bed bound in a matter of months. He required a dedicated team of home healthcare nurses and hospice workers, so a hospital bed was delivered and set up for him in the living room of my grandparent's home. I remember visiting with him frequently as he lay in that bed. I remember his eyes being so sunken and how frail his body looked. He was a mere glimmer of the big, strong man that he had once been. During the summers, my sister and I would spend our days at Grandma and Grandpa's house while Mom was at work. I always looked forward to when Grandpa and I would have our weekly ice cream races at the kitchen table. Grandma would bring two white glass bowls with little handles on them to the table, place them in front of us, and start the countdown. 5 -4- 3- 2- 1…. We would start shoveling heaping spoonfuls of fudge ripple ice milk into our mouths as fast as we could. At some point, he would normally fake an ice cream headache just to let me win and we would just sit and chuckle at ourselves and our accomplishments. After that, he would hold my hand and walk with me to the end of the street where we would wait for my mom to pick me up after work. He had not been able to do any of that after his health started failing, but we still maintained a very special bond as we would sit and talk together for as long as he had the strength.

As the days passed, he continued growing weaker and less communicative until one night I awoke in the middle of the night to find my grandpa standing at the foot of our bed. I remember that he looked so healthy and happy. Dressed in his favorite flannel shirt, he was glowing with a radiant and beautiful peace about him. I remember being curious at his appearance, but also mesmerized. I started to realize that he was not struggling to stand unassisted, and as I glanced down toward the floor, I noticed that he now stood upright on both of his legs. He told me a simple message that he was going to Heaven and to tell my mom that he was okay. With that, he smiled and faded away until all that was left was the silhouette of the bunk beds in the background of the room.

Immediately I woke my mother to tell her what had just happened and what grandpa had said. Half asleep herself, she insisted that I must have been dreaming and she told me to turn over and just go back to sleep. Not five minutes later, the telephone rang, which woke the house in the middle of the night. It was my grandma calling to relay a similar story which she had just experienced. She had seen him at her bedside too, and she wanted my mom to stay on the phone with her while she went into the living room to check on him. Once she got there, she confirmed that he had indeed passed away in his sleep.

My mother began to weep. I can still recall the pain in her voice as she fumbled to try to explain death to a five-year-old child. Most of all, I remember being confused about how sad everyone was since I knew how content my grandpa had been when I had last seen him. As an adult, I still remember him just the way he was when he appeared to me that night. He never did visit me again after that, but that one visit was such an incredible gift to me. Even beyond the comfort that his appearance brought to me as a five-year-old child all those years ago, it has remained a significant source of comfort as I have been forced to continuously grapple with what is waiting on the other side of our current existence. But, if my grandfather's visit was indicative of the best of the other side, then what came next could only represent some of the worst.

During the summer of 1987, my mother bought a nice big home in a better school district on the Northside of Oklahoma City. The house was listed through the United States Department of Housing and Urban Development and beyond being neglected, it had been outright vandalized while it had been sitting vacant over the years. I remember walking through the house and thinking, "We are really going to live here?" It did not really seem like the dream home mom had worked it up to be. Walking through the front door, immediately apparent was a huge six-foot hole in the dining room floor where you could see straight down into the crawl space. Windows had been broken in almost every room, and doors had been kicked or punched in. The house had an old musty smell to it which lingered in every room as we walked through. Despite the condition of the home, it was ours now, and mom immediately hired a crew to come make the necessary repairs so we could move in.

After the repairs, the home was actually very nice, and it was much bigger than our old rental. With a floor plan which included six bedrooms, there was plenty of space for everyone. Having a large family, each of those bedrooms was spoken for. My two aunts had their own individual rooms in the back of the house and my older brother took the converted garage bedroom, while my mom, sister, and I each had our own rooms in the front of the house. My bedroom was situated at the end of a long hall and located between my mother and sister's rooms. Eight years old at the time, my mom had allowed me to pick out my own room color, so I had decided to paint it a light blue shade to match the multicolored blue shag carpet that was already in there. I was happy with my color choice and my room felt like it was just perfect for me!

The first day there was mainly filled with moving in and unpacking. I decided to focus on arranging the things in my bedroom to stay out of the way of the adults. As evening descended on that first day, I grew tired and laid down on the floor of my new room and covered myself up with a throw blanket. Lying quietly in the stillness of the room was a stark contrast to the bustle of excitement I could hear in the rest of the house as everyone continued to work to find new places for all our belongings. As I started to drift off to sleep, I felt an immediate unease roll over me. I could feel a tension in the pit of my stomach and my eyes shot wide open. I looked around the room trying to locate any reason for my reaction, but there was none. Trying to ignore the feeling, I told myself that it was just the new environment, but I knew that I had never felt anything like that before. As exhaustion eventually overtook panic, I fell asleep curled up on the floor, but I never quite got over the unease I felt in that room.

Days turned into months, and months turned to years, and life was going well at our new home. I loved my new school and made friends quickly. I was part of the junior high spirit council team and had made several friends in the youth group at the local Baptist church. Our neighborhood was filled with kids my age, so I was always outside playing and hanging out with them. When I was home, it was mainly only to eat, shower, and sleep. I continued to be minimally disturbed by the strange feeling of being watched while in the front part of the house but having never discovered any reason for the strange feeling, I chose to just try to ignore it.

Around my sophomore year of high school was when I first started to notice it. Just a quick flash of darkness shooting down the hallway. It went by so fast that I could only catch a glimpse of it out of the corner of my eye. I wondered if my eyes were playing tricks on me or if I had even seen anything at all. We had been living in the house for eight years now, and I had never seen anything out of the ordinary at the house during that time. But as the days passed, I continued to catch this shadow darting through my peripheral vision. I was not scared, but more curious about what it could be. I figured that as long as it was not hurting me, there was no harm in it being there. But as its presence continued to grow, I began seeing it more regularly until the sightings were happening multiple times a week. A pattern began to emerge as I noticed that I was seeing it primarily in the evenings, and always in that hallway leading to our bedrooms.

After about a month of elevated activity, I had started noticing that just prior to seeing it, I would get that same knot in the pit of my stomach like I had experienced the very first night in my room. I interpreted it as being almost like an early warning system signaling that the shadow was about to make an appearance. Each time I would get that feeling, I would look up and almost always see it darting by. No matter how quickly I looked, I could never catch it straight on. After about another month, the warning signs began progressing to where I began getting mental visions of the shadow. In my mind's eye, I could never see full details, but could clearly see a more defined image of his shadowy silhouette. He was tall and thin, clothed in a trench coat which hung down to his calves, and he wore a tall fedora hat on his head.

In my day-to-day life, I was a happy and active teenager. I danced in the high school pom squad, sang in show choir, performed in community theater, applied myself academically to my honors courses, attended Vocational-Technical School half a day, and worked part time as a carhop in the evenings. Every Wednesday and Sunday I would attend the local youth group at church after giving my life to Christ at the age of sixteen. To say that I stayed busy would be an understatement. Looking back now, I believe that it may have been my exhaustion which the shadow man thrived on. As I became weaker, it only seemed to grow stronger.

I can clearly remember the first time I saw the shadowy Hat Man straight on in physical form. He had been cohabiting at our home for nine years by then. That evening, I had come home after cheering at one of our high school football games and I was visiting with my mom back in her bedroom. With her bedroom door open, I had a straight view down the hallway from where I was sitting on her bed. We were having a great time together as I was telling her all about the game, when I suddenly got the flash in my mind that He was there. I stopped talking mid-sentence, looked down the hall, and saw his shadow taking slow deliberate steps toward the bedroom. His trench coat swung side to side with each stride, and by the time he had taken about four steps toward me, he disappeared. I looked back at my mom, who had no view of the hallway, and she immediately saw the shock and terror in my eyes. "What did you see?" I replied without hesitation, "A man. A shadow. He was wearing a tall hat."

Upon hearing this, she admitted that she had been noticing shadows too, but had never wanted to say anything since others had not mentioned it. We started asking others in our home about the shadow, and that is when we first started to realize the scope of what had been happening in our home throughout the years.

Numerous times each of us had experienced hearing our names called from a different room only to find that no one had in fact called us. Sometimes it would take the form of mimicking the voices of different family members when it called. We all had also experienced hearing loud bangs from other rooms in the house. At times, this happened with multiple family members present. Each time we would go to investigate the mysterious noise, but there would be no sign of a disturbance. We also began experiencing a phenomenon referred to as apportation, where random objects would disappear and reappear in a different location, or else they would reappear in the expected location at a later time. When these occurrences started gaining in frequency, the temperament of our family slowly began to turn more aggressive towards one another. Seemingly content with the disarray which had been created within the family, it was then that the Hat Man moved into my room to focus all his ill intent on me.

When I was eighteen, I attended nursing school while working full time as a Certified Nursing Assistant at a local nursing home. It was during this time that I experienced the most intense attacks by the Hat Man. I feel silly calling them attacks, because I was never physically harmed, but the mental toll that it took on me at the time was quite severe. Now an adult, I had nonetheless grown afraid of the dark due to his presence, so I bought a TV for my bedroom which I left on all night to provide some sound and light for comfort. He would normally come as I was lying in bed watching a sitcom and trying to settle down for the night. Sometimes I would see a faint shadow, other times I would just feel his presence when he would enter the room. He would normally stand in the corner and stare while putting off the most evil essence I have ever encountered. He was nothing like the gentle spirit of my grandfather and I doubted that the Hat Man was ever human. Most nights I would just lay there terrified and unable to move, tears rolling down my cheeks, while he stood and observed me. Some nights this would last only a few minutes, while other times it could last close to an hour. Once he did leave, I would finally fall asleep and wait for it to all possibly happen again the next night.

Although my mother was always in the next room, I never called for help. To be completely honest, I was incredibly embarrassed to be a young adult and still be so terrified of "the boogeyman." Instead, I turned to prayer and each night I would pray for protection or for God to make the shadow go away. Despite my earnest pleading, night after night my prayers went unanswered. Losing all hope, I felt betrayed and alone and caught in an endless hell where even God would not help me. One of the last nights I remember him visiting, I began praying right after he arrived. Instead of remaining silent like he normally did, he let out a deep guttural growl and shined his red eyes at me from the corner of the room. Suddenly, I started to hear knocking on the walls and fingernails raking down my door. The bangs were coming from all directions around the room when I heard my mother let out a horrified scream from her bedroom next door. I broke free from my fear and ran to her room where I found her hanging approximately two feet out of the bottom of her bed. She explained that something had just grabbed her by the ankles and forcefully pulled her down in the bed. We were both terrified and sat up the rest of the night talking in the living room trying to calm our fears and form a plan. Not knowing what else to do, the next day we blessed each room of the house with holy water and smudged with sage. These actions seemed to calm the activity and we did not suffer any further outright attacks after that night.

Soon after these events, I graduated with my nursing degree and started working twelve-hour overnight shifts at the hospital. Due to my working hours, I never really dealt with Hat Man much after that. This new work schedule may have played a contributing role in the noted decrease in activity we experienced, something I had considered prior to taking the graveyard shift. On the days I wasn't working, I would be out partying so that I could avoid going home where I could possibly have another encounter. At the time I would do anything not to have to face what we had lived through the night of the worst attack. I could still sometimes feel him during the daytime, but there were not any more major nighttime events after that. On one occasion the Hat Man showed a sense of humor, and it was really the only time that I was able to bring myself to laugh at him. I was over twenty-one by the time and I was getting ready to go out to a bar to celebrate Halloween with one of my girlfriends. We had gotten all dressed up and were headed out of the front door when "This is Halloween" from the movie *Nightmare Before Christmas* started blaring loudly throughout the house. It was coming from the direction of my bedroom, so we headed that way to investigate. As we entered the room, we could tell that the sound was coming from the closet. As I reached down to locate the sound, I pulled out an old box, and there amongst the junk was an old alarm clock. Sure enough, it was playing the song at full blast. Once I flipped it over to take out the batteries, the song cut out and quit playing. When I opened the battery panel to remove the batteries, we discovered that it was empty. No batteries. Hat Man took the prize for creepiest Halloween trick that year, and with that, he all but bowed out of our lives.

As activity from Hat Man started to dwindle, I noticed that a new phenomenon had begun taking center stage in my life. I began having very vivid and sometimes downright troubling dreams. Like everyone else, I have had nightmares before, but these were something entirely different. Everything about them was exceedingly real. When I would wake from them, I could recall every precise detail like I had lived through it in my waking life. I later came to understand that what I had started experiencing were prophetic lucid dreams.

The first lucid dream I remember having was just prior to the World Trade Center attack on September 11th. Three separate times I had the same dream sequence where I would witness the scene through what had the appearance of a news report. I would see it from the perspective of walking down a city street with cars parked on the sides of the road and a few people passing by. Each time, everything in my view was covered in gray and ash. I looked up to the sky and saw more ash falling with individual papers floating down in a swaying and drifting motion. The people on the street were all covered in ash, and they were covering their mouths and noses with clothing and rags to keep from inhaling all of the dust in the air. A news ticker streamed across the bottom of the report screen "In the East from the East . . . In the East from the East." The date was displayed in the bottom right corner. It read September 11th.

I knew this dream was different from any I had experienced before so I called a few of my military friends to find out what they knew about any war about to break out. I also made a post online asking if anyone else had been having any weird dreams about World War III. In response, I only got minimal replies. Making light of the situation, my friends would tease me since I was constantly dwelling on it, thinking that the government must be hiding something. It honestly went beyond anxiety and teetered on paranoia for a few weeks leading up to the attack. Then the morning of September 11th came. I had just completed my third consecutive twelve-hour night shift and had come home to get some much-needed sleep. Even though I had previously been anxious about that day, it had not occurred to me what day it was. As I had just laid down in my bed, my brother called and asked "Are you watching this? A plane just hit the World Trade Center." I flipped it over to the national news and started watching. It still was not evident to me that this is what I had been dreaming about until I saw the now familiar view being broadcast. It was like Deja vu for me, but everyone I knew could confirm that this was the exact scene which I had been talking about for the past couple of weeks. One of my military friends ended up calling me that morning after discussing what was happening with a few others and one of them brought up the dreams I had been having. One of their superiors got on the phone and asked me what else I knew, but at that point they knew as much as I did. Leading up to that day, I never saw any planes, I had no idea who Osama Bin Laden was, and I never saw the buildings fall, but I was certain that there would be a crowded city street covered in ash.

After Sept 11th, I experienced a couple more precognitive dreams. In one, I saw the Pope passing away and black smoke rising into the sky. In another, I saw a whole city being flooded while I rode a canoe through murky, contaminated water. About a week later, Hurricane Katrina hit New Orleans and we watched as people struggled to get out of the city. After that, I never really had that type of dream again. The phenomenon came on out of nowhere and left just as quickly.

A young adult by this time, I soon moved out on my own and rented a small apartment in the heart of Oklahoma City. I continued to work overnight shifts at the hospital three nights a week, and on this day, I had just finished my third shift in a row. As was sometimes my habit following my final shift of the week, I chose to forego sleep that morning to run some important errands during the daytime hours. Finally returning home that evening, I collapsed onto the couch to watch T.V., exhausted from having been awake for over twenty-four hours straight. Within minutes I had drifted off into a much-needed sleep.

Sometime later, I remember suddenly being aware of standing in the corner of the living room. Confused, I stood motionless, visually searching my surroundings to try to understand what was happening. I noticed that the atmosphere of the apartment seemed distorted and shrouded in shadow. Glancing directly across the room, I recognized my couch and noticed my body lying face down with my face buried in the cushions. Strangely, this sight did not bother me. Instead, the feeling that surrounded me was one of peace and inquisitiveness. I knew that the girl on the couch was me, and I loved her and fully accepted her current state as being natural. Above me, I saw a warm amber-white light glowing in the distance. Beautiful sparkles of gold fell towards me through the soft beam. I looked back over at my body still face down on the couch, and that is when I heard a knock on my door.

Now focused on the door, I watched from the corner of the room as one of my high school friends emerged through the solid surface. I wondered what he was doing here, as he had passed away a few years ago. Ignoring my presence in the corner, he was focused on my lifeless body. "Mindy! Mindy!" he called lightheartedly. "Mindy! Get up!" Seeing no response, he made a strange face showing a mixture of concern and happiness then proceeded to run full force at me throwing his elbow up in the air and slamming down onto me in a playful way. At this, I awoke with a jolt, and immediately I realized I was in trouble.

I had fallen asleep on my stomach with my hands folded under my body and my face buried into one of the couch cushions. Both of my arms were completely asleep underneath me, so I could not muster the strength needed to push myself up and turn over. Struggling to take in any amount of desperately needed oxygen, I was able to turn my head just enough to be able to "sip" air from the small space around my face above the cushion. This gave me the imperative energy to be able to throw my left leg backwards over my body with enough force to flip myself over onto the floor between the couch and coffee table. I landed with a thud.

The first breath to enter my lungs caused me to begin choking and coughing as my body struggled to accept the much-needed air. I laid there on the floor regaining my strength and trying to compose my thoughts for a good half hour, then, I did what any twenty-something girl would do in this kind of situation, I called my mom. Luckily, I had the kind of relationship with my mother where I could talk to her about things like this. To this day, I am still not sure if I had a true Near-Death Experience that day. Although it certainly had many of the expected elements, I feel deep down that it was more of an out of body experience which was encountered while in a very dangerous life-threatening situation, and not a full-on crossing over event. Unlike my NDE following the vertebral artery dissection, I did not experience the NDE related aftereffects following this event, but of course, I did continue to experience phenomena stemming from the underlying encounter prone personality.

A few years later, I was asked to spend a week house-sitting for some of my military friends. (Names are changed to protect their identities.) Each of them happened to be on temporary duty or on leave during this one particular week. I had been working agency assignments at the hospital in that town quite frequently, so they asked me to stay there at the house for a few days to keep an eye on the place in their absence. It was a great arrangement for me since it meant that I did not have to drive all the way back to the city each day after my shift, so I happily agreed. These guys were like brothers to me, and I spent so much time with them that their house was almost like a second home. The first day I arrived for house sitting duty I went back to Jay's room where I placed my suitcase and scrubs since he tended to be the tidiest of the bunch. I grabbed a blanket and a pillow and headed for the couch to settle in for an evening of vegging out in front of the T.V.

Later that night as I was starting to get sleepy, the television in Caleb's room turned on. His room was at the end of the hall and was in my direct line of sight from where I was sitting on the couch. Intrigued, I walked down the hall, flipped on his light, and turned off his T.V. I reasoned that perhaps he had a timer set for some unknown reason, so I did not pay it much mind. I turned out the light and headed back to the couch. By the time I sat down, the T.V. in Caleb's room had turned itself on once again. This time it slightly unnerved me, but I knew that I had to go back in there and turn it off. So down the hall I went again, turned on the light, turned off the T.V., turned the light off, and hurried back to the couch. I slightly held my breath as I sat down expecting the television to switch on again, but to my relief it stayed silent this time. I tried not to let the strange sequence of events bother me too much, so I started my movie back up and eventually I was able to drift off to sleep.

In my dream state, I found myself lying on the couch when I saw the television in Caleb's room turn on again. Just as had happened in real life, I got up to turn it off, but this time as I passed Jay's room, I saw a woman sitting on his bed. She had long curly brown hair, fiery red lips, pale skin, and a short red sequined dress. She was beautiful, but in an almost trashy kind of way. I leaned into the room and asked her what she was doing there and let her know that no one was supposed to be there while the guys were out of town. She just smiled and mockingly said "Oh, I just come to f*** the guys from time to time." She then threw her head back in what can only be described as typical evil fashion and started laughing maniacally. Between each breath, the diabolical laughter progressively became deeper and deeper in pitch until the sound of it turned into something sounding fully demonic. At that, I sensed very real danger and turned to run, but the infernal woman caught me by the throat and strangled me tighter and tighter as I struggled against her. The encounter was so frightening that once I realized I was in a dream state, I forced myself to wake up. I did not know what would happen if she won, and it was apparent that in that state, I was not strong enough to fight her off.

I awoke with a large gasp. I struggled to still myself given the battle I had just endured. As I laid on the couch trying to catch my breath, I immediately realized that I could hear the chatter from the television in Caleb's room again. At this point I was ready to leave, but all of my belongings, and most importantly my car keys, were in the room where I had just seen her. It was about 4:30 AM, so being a smoker at the time, I grabbed my pack of cigarettes and went outside to sit on the porch to wait for a much-welcomed sunrise.

Once daylight broke, I worked up a bit of courage to reenter the house. I readied myself, ran in, turned off the T.V., grabbed my things, and left within about a thirty second time frame. Once safely in my car, I called Caleb to see if any of them had ever noticed strange things in that house. At first, he did not recall anything strange, but once I started describing what had happened, he was in disbelief. He told me that he had been having nightmares and had repeatedly suffered attacks from the same woman which I had seen in Jay's room. He had even asked the other guys about it, and while they did not confirm or deny it, they did not want to discuss the subject. After that night, I continued to go by and check on the house until one of the guys returned home from leave. Once Caleb returned, he chose to pack up his belongings and move out of the house. This was my only run in with what I believe was a succubus type of entity and I never did return to the house after my encounter there. Shortly afterwards, the rest of the guys left the house for good as the service called them to different assignment locations.

Following these encounters and desperate to understand my tendency to attract and experience unexplained phenomena, I sought out the paranormal community. I started reading books about hauntings and took a local ghost tour where I quickly became friends with the owner of the company. Within weeks, I ended up joining her team of investigators and went on several haunting investigations around our state. In an effort to answer my own questions surrounding the identity and origin of these different types of entities, I applied myself to the use of electronic voice phenomenon. Known as EVP, it is a technique used to capture and record spirit voices and I figured it was my best bet at trying to make contact and receive answers. I had encountered human spirits, but I knew there were other types of beings out there too, and I believed that they were possibly using similar doors to manifest and communicate in our dimension. The Hat Man and the apparent succubus were neither one very nice, but they both seemed so vastly different in too many ways to be the same type of entity. I questioned if these were all unique types of entities, why did I keep encountering them when most people will go their whole lives without ever seeing one single ghost? Was there something about me that left me open to these phenomena? If I didn't have so many witnesses to these different events, I would have questioned my own sanity. And even with that validation, I still sought to gather proof of their existence.

Continuing my search for answers, I happened to come across a local pastor online and we began talking. After a few weeks, we scheduled a date and met up to discuss some of these beings which I had come across over the years. As a Christian, I desperately wanted to get a well thought out religious perspective on my experiences. Pastor John and I didn't always agree on what different scriptures meant, but I really appreciated the way that he would admit when he did not know something. Instead, he would very patiently try to help me find answers to my many questions. We had so many great discussions and had begun meeting up so often that we quickly began dating. I loved the way that he always challenged me and the way that we continued to learn about new things together. He was always so supportive of me and never made me feel bad about the supernatural happenings which had become such a normal part of my life. Little did he know that he would soon get a front row seat at the next otherworldly event.

It was in the early days of our dating life when I started noticing a spirit around me named Anna. I never really had a spirit follow me around like that before, but she had a pleasantness about her that put me at ease while obviously piquing my curiosity. I would notice her dropping in from time to time throughout the day and I found it somewhat curious how suddenly she had shown up. Searching my mind for clues about her about her origin, my best guess was maybe she had found me at one of the hospitals in which I had recently worked. The thought had never crossed my mind that her appearance may be related to the man who would soon become my husband.

The first time John took me out to the family farm to meet his father, I was surprised to discover that Anna was there. After spending the morning visiting and getting a tour of the farm, John and his father went out to the barn to work on the combine while I went into one of the bedrooms to take a nap since I had worked an overnight shift the previous evening. Once I was alone in the bedroom, I felt the familiar spirit of Anna in the room, but another presence arrived soon after. His name was Victor, and he was talking to Anna……about me. It was immediately apparent that they knew each other! She was telling Victor all about me "Isn't she pretty? This is John's new girlfriend. She's a nurse." He just stood next to her and agreed as she spoke. I could also feel the presence of others gathered around the room, but those two were the ones who were most prominent. It was then that I started to realize that Anna must be connected to John in some way. As they continued to talk and express their approval of me, I drifted off to sleep. While the situation could come off as a bit creepy, for me, it was all actually very sweet and endearing. I instantly felt accepted and loved by all of the family at the farm.

After my nap, I got up and went outside to find the guys still tinkering with the farm equipment out in the barn. I pulled John aside and asked if he had any idea who Victor and Anna were. He was curious and somewhat confused, "Well we have both a Victor and an Anna in our family, but they have both passed away. Victor was my grandpa and Anna was his mom, my great grandma." He went on to tell me how Victor had been raised on that land and worked the farm for over fifty years before handing it down to the next generation. That farm had been in the family for five generations, and it was only fitting that all the family would still be gathered there and looking out for each other. After that visit, Anna remained on the farm instead of following me, but I would still feel her spirit around sometimes when we visited. It is amazing to think that it is possible to feel the love that our ancestors have for us from beyond the veil, but that is exactly what I feel every time we visit my husband's childhood home.

It was not long before our small family of two began to grow. John and I had our son JJ during the first year of our marriage, followed shortly thereafter by our beautiful daughter Aneshka. Those years were filled with such wonderful memories as we matured together and watched our children live through their many milestone firsts. I wholeheartedly loved the life we had built together and there was a palpable sense of joy that filled our home. We moved around a bit due to John's job as a pastor, but we were always so happy to have one another. I had a few minor paranormal events happen during that time, but for the most part, we lived a quiet life with minimal unexplained encounters while the children were young. There was ongoing, but sporadic spirit activity like one time when I was going into the nursery to check on our son when I heard a woman's voice loudly exclaim with a British accent "We watch over the baby!" There was also an instance when I had a visit from a church member's husband who had passed away. There were also some frightening experiences including when I had vivid dreams in which I struggled against an unseen force while my spirit was thrashed around the ceiling. While the encounters were lessened for the five-year span, they were very much still there.

Visiting my mother's home during those years, we would occasionally still encounter the shadow man. To this day, she and both of my aunts still live in that house. From a young age, each of our children has sensed something dark in that part of the house despite the family never revealing our past experiences to them. The last time I had a run in with the shadow was around 2010 when John and I, along with both of our children, had come to town to visit my family and we had decided to stay overnight there. My aunt gave me a set of sheets to make up the bed in the guest room which had been my sister's old bedroom. I walked into the room and placed the sheets on the bed when I suddenly heard John come up behind me and whisper something into my ear. I could feel his nose in my hair and his breath on my skin, but I could not quite make out what he said. I almost thought I had understood his words, but what I thought I heard made absolutely no sense. I turned around to ask him what he meant and that is when I realized that John was never actually there. The words now made perfect sense in this new context. "Better say a prayer." I ran out of there very upset and told John what had just happened. He helped calm my fears, then helped me make up the bed together so I would not have to be in there alone. Although we made it through the rest of the night uneventfully, that was the last time we stayed overnight in that part of my mother's home.

Shadow People, prankster spirits, entity attacks, out of body experiences, ghost encounters, and prophetic dreams; these are just a sampling of the types of unusual encounters I regularly experienced while growing up. Taken as a collective, it is easy to discern why the term encounter-prone would be quite fitting. I can understand how those who have never had such an encounter could read these accounts and think me unhinged, but I would ask them to bear in mind that deficiency of personal experience does not invalidate the experiences of others, nor does it rule out the existence of things which one has not encountered. Although I do not agree with many of his viewpoints, I can find infinite value in one statement made by the nineteenth century German philosopher Friedrich Nietzsche, "And those who were seen dancing were thought to be insane by those who could not hear the music." What a fitting analogy for such a situation. I aspire that all who have not had occasion to experience such extraordinary phenomena would one day hear the music.

Chapter 7

Experiencing After Effects

"You must be the change you wish to see in the world."
- Mahatma Gandhi

Along with the Encounter Prone Personality, Dr. Ring was able to identify several aftereffects which were commonly reported by those claiming to have had either a UFO Encounter or a Near-Death Experience. He divided these traits into two categories: Psychological and Physiological. In this chapter, I would like to look at these more in depth, then focus on each individually as they relate to my personal journey.

The psychological effects included having a defining line of separation between the former self and the new self which emerged following the encounter. Most felt they had a new life purpose and that they now understood the big picture relating to all of existence. Experiencers also reported having a new and deep understanding that they were an immortal soul temporarily living in a physical realm. Many emerged from their experiences with a life mission of extending universal love to others. They became more generous and cared more deeply for humanity, animals, and the Earth. Those who were religious before their encounter, along with those who were not, both experienced a shift toward spirituality and reported increased psychic abilities. These abilities included out of body experiences and encounters with Non-Human Intelligences including both spirits and extraterrestrials amongst other types.

On the physiological side, both UFO Experiencers and Near-Death Experiencers reported an increase in photosensitivity and noise sensitivity following their encounter. They also noted changes to their health which included increased susceptibility to allergies, electrical sensitivities, and a younger looking appearance. Both NDE and UFO respondents reported changes to their life approach which included the use of alternative healthcare, as well as diet and lifestyle changes. A noted amount also experienced shifts in their relationships and career tracks. Incredibly, a handful of respondents also claimed to now possess the ability to heal.

I began experiencing common aftereffects almost immediately following my NDE, although I did not understand what they were at the time. Many will recognize several of the resulting effects as ones which I was facing during my recovery period as described in Chapters 3 and 4 of this book. Some of the physiological symptoms I experienced were already somewhat normal for me relating to my now identified encounter prone personality as well as my already weakened physical state. I had battled severe photosensitivity since my teens because of the faulty connective tissue in my eyes and I suffered from multiple lifelong food and environmental allergies. Both have been identified as highly reported aftereffects following an NDE, but for me, there was a small, noted increase in their severity. Although I had lost most of my hearing during the Vertebral Artery Dissection, noise sensitivity always was and still remains the most severe physiological after effect which I continue to endure.

The first physiological effect I noticed, and somewhat jokingly started attributing to my brush with death, was the ability to affect electronics. I first noticed it several months after my dissection while driving down an empty road in northern Oklahoma one night. John was behind the wheel, and I was riding in the passenger seat since I was still nearly losing consciousness quite frequently. I was not feeling well that night and I remember suffering from car sickness which was abnormal for me. While we were driving down the road, the streetlights above us went out one after another, after another, in sequence as we passed below them. As we would emerge out from under each one, they would flicker and return to full brightness. I remember counting no less than seven lights which went out seemingly on cue. I joked that it must be due to my "psychic powers" since John still did not know about my NDE at the time. This encounter always seemed odd to me, and I filed it away in the back of my mind because I felt in my spirit that it may in some way be related to the power released in my body during my return from the other side.

Shortly after the street light incident, I had a couple of encounters with microwaves which either completely quit working once I touched them, or glitched so badly that the appliance did not function properly following my contact with the machine. As interesting as those encounters were, most of my problems with technology showed up after the Coronavirus pandemic hit in 2019. It was a time when most of the world was now forced into figuring out how to connect with others through somewhat new mediums such as online conferencing services. While these platforms were already widely available, most people did not utilize them regularly outside of business settings. That all changed as we as a worldwide society looked for new ways to connect with loved ones and meet new friends in a safe online environment.

At the time we were living in Oklahoma City, and I had been faithfully meeting with my counselor Michelle every week. With her help, I had been able to begin working through some of the effects of the physical trauma which I had endured, but all of that came to a halt with lockdowns suddenly in full swing. With John now aware of my NDE, we looked for new ways to connect with others who might understand and possibly even relate to my encounter. That is exactly what we found in an organization named the International Association for Near-Death Studies, or IANDS. Their website describes the founding of the 501c3 Organization as follows:

> The pioneering work of psychiatrists Elisabeth Kübler-Ross, Raymond Moody, Jr. and George Ritchie brought Near-Death Experiences to public attention in the 1970's. During the years that followed, research studies by Kenneth Ring, PhD, Michael Sabom, MD, Bruce Greyson, MD, and others extended the early findings and stimulated additional interest in the field.
>
> To meet the needs of early researchers and experiencers, IANDS was founded in 1978 and incorporated in Connecticut in 1981. It was the first organization in the world devoted to the study of near-death and similar experiences and their relationship to human consciousness. Today its varied membership represents every continent but the Antarctic. (IANDS, History and Founders, 2017)

After doing more research into the organization, John discovered that they regularly offered "IANDS Sharing Groups

Online" which was open to those who had experienced an NDE, their loved ones, and anyone from the general public with an interest in the subject. The sharing groups appeared to be a perfect platform for me to connect with others who had gone through similar struggles. We excitedly signed up for the next meeting that week, but part of me was terrified. I was not sure what to expect and did not want to find myself pressured into sharing my experience if I did not feel safe and ready to share it with others. Despite my anxiety, I knew that this was my best chance at finally beginning the long journey through understanding what had happened to me and processing any meaning that could be drawn from it. I wanted to be brave, but I feared letting others know the horrible anguish I had suffered on the other side. What would they think of me? Would they think I had gotten exactly what I deserved? Would they judge me for not having a Heavenly experience? As I went to bed that night, these thoughts swirled through my mind. I was restless to say the least. It was right as I found myself in the state just between wakefulness and sleep that I noticed a familiar and comforting face coming into view.

Quite unexpectedly, my Grandmother Eunice had come for a visit. For years she had been the matriarch of our family and was greatly loved by all that knew her. She passed away just prior to my nineteenth birthday, and I had missed her presence through so many milestones in my life. You can understand my amazement when she came to me in spirit form all these years after her death. Strangely enough, I was not alarmed by her appearance, but instead, I embraced it immediately as a welcome reunion. I had never had such a strong spirit encounter in all my years, and it seems silly to me now that I did not instantly understand the magnitude and importance of her arrival.

Her spirit first relayed to me how happy she was that I had married a preacher, "Just like her daddy." She loved John and knew how well he had taken care of me through all of my health struggles. She then spoke about JJ sharing how handsome and smart she thought he was. She saved Aneshka for last. She was so taken with the person my daughter was turning out to be. She commented that Aneshka reminded her of me when I was a child with how caring yet ornery she was, just the right mix of sweetness and sass. She had enjoyed watching our little family grow and was so proud of all of us. It was a wonderful visit, and it came to an end way too quickly for my liking. As she was speaking, she started fading from view, but before she was gone, she held out a handful of yellow flowers in a very meaningful gesture. I am not one who is well versed in botany. I do not do any gardening or know flowers by sight, so I asked, "What flowers are those?" Her last words before she was gone came clearly, "They are Yellow Daisies." At this, I forced myself to wake up enough to type "Yellow Daisies" into my phone before quickly falling asleep.

The next morning, my first thought was of Grandma Eunice's visit. I excitedly picked up my cell phone to check it, and right there in front of me was my note from the night before. Yellow Daisies. There had to be a meaning behind why Grandma had chosen to hold those specific flowers out to me. It just seemed too random to not have been a message of some kind that she was wanting to relay. I opened my web browser and performed a search for meanings behind what the flowers could symbolize. There was a common consensus throughout several of the websites I checked which pointed to yellow daisies being a symbol of joy and happiness. "How sweet," I thought, but deep down in my soul I still felt like I had to be missing something. I knew I would have to keep searching. Since I had a full day of errands ahead of me, plus I was planning to attend the IANDS meeting later that day, I decided to do a deeper dive into flower meanings later that week. I was determined to figure out why Grandma Eunice had chosen to come to me at this time and why she had decided to share this intriguing cryptic message.

That evening John and I set up our laptop and logged online to attend our first IANDS Sharing Group meeting. Instantly we began having problems with connectivity as the screen would freeze multiple times and a warning would display stating that our connection was unstable. It was a problem I had been noticing quite frequently when working on my MUFON cases. John had even bought me a new laptop computer to try to remedy the problem, yet it persisted. We had even tried using his computer, but it seemed any time I was nearby, any computer would start having connectivity problems. We had paid to have the best internet service available in our area since John and the kids were now doing school from home. No one else had connection problems during this time. The problem was so bad that during my video conferences, we would have everyone in our home turn off their devices including all phones, televisions, tablets, and gaming systems so as not to interfere with my internet connection.

As it became increasingly clear that these issues were related directly to me, we discovered that the electrical and connectivity problems I had been experiencing were often related to NDE aftereffects. We also noticed an obvious correlation between the severity of the disruptions and the status of my emotional state. Phone and internet connectivity tended to get much worse for me as my emotions escalated. As you can imagine, this presented a huge problem since I was dealing with PTSD, and I was attempting to attend a meeting about a highly charged emotional subject.

Fortunately, we were able to get the connection stable enough to hear most of our first IANDS Sharing Group meeting. It was well moderated, and they allowed each person a chance to speak as they felt led. I struggled through most of it as I listened to others discuss the wonderful things they had experienced after crossing over. While I know I should have been happy for them and their great experiences, all I could think about was how wretched I must have been to be the only one there who had such a dark experience. I felt overwhelming shame and turned off my camera multiple times to collect myself. This meeting was so much harder than I thought it was going to be, yet I knew that I was right where I needed to be. At the end of the meeting, and with John by my side, the moderator offered me a chance to share my experiences. Knowing that I was in a safe space, I summoned up all the courage I had, and through many heavy tears, I spoke about my time in the Void.

The group listened quietly as many showed signs of love and support through hand gestures held up to their cameras and head nods of understanding. Some cried right along with me, while others sent out a flood of hearts across the screen. As I finished speaking, one of the beautiful souls who was helping to moderate the meeting reached in front of her where there was a mason jar with a single yellow flower. I had not even noticed it earlier during the course of the meeting. I watched in amazement as she took the flower out of its humble container and held it up lovingly to the camera using the same gesture as Grandma Eunice. Seeing this, I completely lost it as a wave of realization washed over me.

In that instance I undoubtedly received the full message which my grandmother wanted to relay to me the night before. Not only was she aware that I was going to be in that IANDS meeting, but she was fully aware of why I would be attending it. This means that she knew I had been to the other side. More importantly, she knew about the soul crushing time that I had spent in the solitude in the Void. With her message now exceedingly clear, I began understanding that maybe I was not so alone over there after all. Maybe my loved ones did come to greet me, but for whatever reason, I was not able to perceive them. I have no doubts to this very day that this is the message she so lovingly wanted to convey. Her gracious gesture is the sole reason I am now able to speak so openly about my NDE and I believe that is what she wanted; for my soul to begin healing in the knowledge that I am deeply loved. It is a message I needed to receive in order to comfort me and to enable me to speak about my experience with others. I knew that this meeting was just the first of many times where I would need to share my NDE with others and it was a great first step in finding my voice.

The disruptive computer interferences I encountered (which remain ongoing) and the spirit meeting with my grandmother unfolded within 24 hours of each other and they represent two aftereffects commonly reported following a Near-Death Experience. The next major after effect I noticed happened while we were once again house hunting. The pandemic had given us plenty of time to assess our home amenities and with two kids quickly approaching their teen years, we knew that they were not meeting our current needs. Home interest rates plummeted to the lowest they had been in decades, so we began looking to upgrade to a bigger home with an in-ground swimming pool. We wanted a home where our kids would want to spend their free time and would feel free to invite their friends over. The pool would also offer the added benefit of allowing me to exercise without putting too much strain on my joints while working to regain my core body strength. Without a second thought, we put our house on the market and set out to find our forever home where we could finally settle down.

Unbeknownst to us, the great post-pandemic housing rush had begun as it seemed almost everyone else in the United States had come up with the same plan to upgrade their living conditions during this time. The house we owned had multiple showings and sold for well over our listing price the first day it was on the market. The problem then became finding a home which met our needs and getting an offer in on it before the homeowner took an all-cash offer well above what any lender would approve. This same scenario played out repeatedly as we would get our hopes up that we had finally landed a home, only to find out that we had lost it to another cash offer from out of state. We made offers on seven different homes during that time and although we would be the top offer as we went to bed each time, we would wake up the next day to see each home listed as "Sold" on the real estate website. With the pressure of having a closing date on the house we were selling quickly approaching, we were forced to begin looking at homes that were a bit of an upgrade but did not offer an in-ground pool or other amenities we were hoping for. With each passing day, home prices continued to soar and what was in reach the day before suddenly became out of our budget amid fierce bidding wars.

With all these factors in place, our realtor suggested that we look at a home which had been newly listed and had the most opulent upgrades you could imagine for a home in our price range. Pulling up outside the house, you could not miss the finely manicured fescue lawn with blades all exactly the same length and a beautifully manicured garden area. It was immediately evident that this would have been the fanciest house we had ever owned. Walking inside the front door, the home was breathtaking. It had custom hand-blown glass chandeliers throughout, a newly remodeled kitchen with top-of-the-line appliances, and a bathroom to die for. Despite all of this, I stood frozen at the front door as soon as I stepped foot in the house. I instantly tried to turn around and leave, but our realtor must have noticed my face and she put her hand on my back to guide me further into the home. I turned to her and told her, "I do not like this house. Something is off."

She was taken aback since the home was one of the nicer ones we had viewed, and we had put in offers on houses that were not as nice as this one. She persuaded me to walk through the house and see all of it before making a final decision as to if we would like to make an offer on it. With every step I took through the home, I could feel myself trembling and my stomach becoming sick. I wanted nothing to do with this place and I had no idea why I was reacting so negatively, but I trusted my instincts. I felt somewhat silly being a grown woman and acting this way. We grabbed our kids from the backyard where they had instinctively gone instead of checking out the home like they normally would do, and we quickly left without putting in an offer. We looked at a few other homes afterwards, but my strong reaction to the beautiful home was still gnawing at me.

Returning home, I knew that I had to do some digging to find out if there was any known reason why I may have been so repulsed by this house. I did a brief online search for the home address to see if maybe any violent crimes had occurred there. It was a newer home, so I was even open to the possibility that something could have been tied to the land. After several hours of searching, I came up empty and I almost chalked the whole episode up to just the incredible amount of stress we had been under, but then John suggested that I search the names of the previous property owners. Here is where my strong negative intuition about the place finally gained some clarity. The previous owner had spent decades in prison for heinous crimes against a child. My heart sank as I read about it, and I knew then that my repulsion of that place was justified. I had never experienced any intuitive abilities on this scale before my NDE, but I believe it served to guide us away from a home saturated with negative energy from one of the worst kinds of evil man has ever committed.

It was not long after viewing that house that our realtor got a call informing us that we had landed a specific home which we had been hoping for all along! It was one of the first homes we had looked at, and we had absolutely fallen in love with. The home was warm and welcoming, and it felt like we were meant to be there from the second we stepped in the door. Unfortunately for us, the owners initially bypassed our offer and they had instead accepted a cash offer from an out of state buyer. Since our offer was a solid one, we were kept as the backup in case things fell through with the first guy, and that is exactly what ended up happening. We ended up landing our dream home that embodied nearly everything we had wanted in a lifelong family home. Within several weeks, we had successful closings on both our old and new home, and eagerly began moving into our new place. It seemed that everything in my life was being laid out for me and I was so grateful for the amazing upgrades that were taking place in every facet of my life.

Once we had unpacked all the moving boxes and all our knickknacks had found a place on the gorgeous built-in shelves that lined the walls of our new home, John and I turned our attention to finally taking a deep dive into learning more about Near-Death Experiences. In particular, we wanted to learn everything we could about distressing NDEs and any meaning which had been derived from others who had experienced one. Even though our family had been going through another major adjustment period including the recent move, John graduating with his Master of Education degree, as well as him searching for a new administrative position at work, the slower pace of life we had become accustomed to during the pandemic allowed us some time to learn and grow together.

It was obvious that each of us was struggling with where we stood spiritually in light of what my encounter had revealed and how it measured up against what we had been taught growing up in church. Since most churches had moved to an online format at the beginning of the lockdowns, we no longer felt compelled to attend every Sunday service as we would have once religiously done. This gave us the freedom to explore other interpretations of the scripture and other belief systems which could help better explain what I had experienced. I do not know if I can fully convey what a struggle it was for us as fundamentalist Christians to acknowledge and accept the validity of other doctrines outside of what we had previously staunchly believed. It was not an easy process for either of us, let alone factoring in the major transition it was for our children. This was one of the main things I had heavily worried about when first sharing my NDE with my family, but as we searched for answers together, I was able to quickly see the positive effects this new open mindedness was having on each of us.

We had become more accepting and forgiving of others, and even more so, more forgiving of ourselves with every passing day. Our children were able to begin opening up to us about their own struggles. They were growing secure in the knowledge that we would fully accept them as they were, something which may not have happened if we had held tightly to our previous belief system. We were now able to speak with each other more openly about our feelings without reserve or fear of being looked down upon. While most of the NDE aftereffects had only affected me, this move toward a more spiritual mindset, as opposed to one of any one organized religion, was one of the most significant transformations we experienced together as a family. Over the years following my experience, we have each grown spiritually stronger and more assured of the importance and miracle of our existence which no doubt continues after this life.

Shortly after our move, our family also collectively began noticing strange shadows and light anomalies around our home. This is something which was new to John and JJ, but we all encountered these plays of light in the years following my NDE. At first, we thought maybe it could be attributed to the new setting and needing to become more familiar with the way the natural light fell in the home, but that was quickly ruled out as these lights and shadows performed movements which were not naturally possible. Some would take the form of orbs of light, some would be seen zipping through open doorways, and others could be seen bending down hallways, all things which natural light does not typically do.

On the flip side, we were also seeing unexplained shadow anomalies in our home quite regularly. One of the more astonishing shadow displays was seen one afternoon while John and I were sitting together in our sunken living room. An activity that he and I immensely enjoy is reading through books together. We will take turns sharing chapters aloud followed by a lively discussion of our thoughts on the subject as we progress through each section. This is exactly what we were doing one day during the spring of 2021. I was curled up on the couch across the room from John with my back toward our large picture window while John was sitting on the loveseat facing me and reading aloud as we worked our way through *Dancing Past the Dark* by Nancy Evans Bush. (This important book is described in detail in Chapter 8). Her NDE experience was extremely similar to my own in that she also visited the Void, but in her experience, it prominently featured black and white Yin-Yang symbols.

We were nearing the end of the book where she was speaking about the need for the theme of darkness versus light, so I was listening intently and working to mentally apply these new concepts and insights to my own NDE. I had found such comfort in her words during our readthrough since it was the first time I had found someone else who completely understood what I had experienced. Suddenly, a line of dark shadow appeared covering the full expanse of our living room which is approximately thirty feet in length. The darkness started at the ground level and in one steady motion, it receded up the wall and across the ceiling. It continued on the other side of the room as it began descending the opposite wall, finally terminating as it reached the large picture window. John, engrossed in reading, began noticing the change in light as the shadow was lifting on the wall behind him and once it had reached the ceiling, he stopped reading to inquire what was happening. We watched together as it performed maneuvers which would have been impossible for a light being cast in from our window, and even though we knew this, we sat and tried to find some reasonable explanation for what we had just seen.

With the large window facing our backyard, we thought maybe something could have cast a shadow into the window by flying overhead, but that was quickly dismissed since our patio is sheltered by a large, covered pergola which extends out about ten feet from our roof and blocks any light from being directed straight down. We also have an eight-foot-tall privacy fence which blocks any light from being cast from the street. Then there is the problem of the light being cast up onto the ceiling and on the wall directly above the picture window. After living in this house for a couple of years, we still have not been able to find any reasonable explanation for what we witnessed that day and we have never seen a similar display like it again. We feel that the experience was a symbolic "lifting of the veil" relating to the texts which we were reading at the time and another gentle nudge from loved ones on the other side pointing us to a better understanding of my experiences in the Void.

While we did not witness any further shadow anomalies of that magnitude in the home, other phenomena became commonplace. We all have witnessed light orbs flying through the house. Normally they are illuminated white to blue-white in color. They will sometimes be seen zipping through the house quickly on a straight path, and other times they seem to meander through, zigzagging around before fading out. We also frequently experience doors opening and closing on their own. This has happened with all our bedroom doors, but thankfully, the phenomenon has left our exterior and bathroom doors alone to date. During one Zoom meeting for the Iowa - Nebraska MUFON chapter, I had signed on to watch a presentation by Preston Dennet, only to get in about fifteen minutes and have my bedroom door opened approximately three inches. I distinctly heard a man's voice utter an inquisitive "Hello?' before pulling the door completely shut again. I instantly shut off my camera and jumped up to see if John or JJ needed something, but upon checking, JJ and Aneshka were each still in bed asleep, and John was out running errands that morning. It seemed to be just another event in a long string of encounters which had become all too commonplace lately. Just the week before, Aneshka had been awoken in the night by footsteps in her bedroom followed by the door on her armoire unlatching and swinging widely open.

I also had a bizarre encounter one day while John and the kids were off at school. I was sitting alone in the living room working on some of my cases when I suddenly heard a low-pitched warbling noise in both of my ears. The sound seemed to penetrate my body and I felt the vibration throughout my skull. A voice then audibly told me inside my head, "Do not freak out. This will only take a minute." I did not recognize the voice as being my own, or the random thought as originating from myself. This has been the only time I experienced something like this, and I did not notice any missing time in conjunction with this experience. It was quite out of the ordinary compared to other encounters I had previously experienced, and I think that is why it unnerved me so much.

If there is any practical explanation for this event, then I am sure an argument could be made that it was caused by some kind of interference relating to my hearing aids. With that in mind, I can say that I have never had them malfunction before in such a manner and that the noise did not seem to be emanating from the hearing aid units, only filtered through them. It is a noted difference that I deal with every day, and I am skilled in deciphering between someone speaking in the room I am in, versus someone speaking in a video that I am playing through the hearing aids. The sound comes through differently depending on where the sound originates. Nonetheless, this remains one of the more abnormal encounters which I experienced following my NDE and which I still cannot fully explain. After the first year at our new house, these encounters, including light anomalies and interactions with doors opening and closing steeply decreased inside our home, but the aftereffects continued in other respects.

In July 2022, I attended the MUFON International Symposium in Las Vegas, NV where I was scheduled to be a speaker for the 2021 Top Cases of Interest presentation. Reserved for the end of the three-day conference, this presentation focused on some of the more interesting cases which had been reported to MUFON throughout the previous year. I had been fortunate enough to have had an amazing case come into the Oklahoma MUFON chapter and it had been deemed the 2021 Case of the Year. It featured a group of young students and their teacher who all witnessed a large saucer shaped craft descend over their small rural boarding school in the mid-1970s. The case had stirred up quite a bit of attention since it bore so many similarities to other well-known schoolyard encounters such as the

1966 Australian Westall High School sighting and the 1994 Ariel School encounter in Zimbabwe.

Having been a housewife and nurse prior to this, I had no previous public speaking experience and had battled terrible social anxiety my whole life. While I was honored and excited to have the opportunity to present this case which I was proud of, inside my mind I was locked in a state of pure panic. I tried to push through the weekend and hide my anxiety, but it seems that some aspects of my extreme state could not be hidden. I had copied my slideshow onto a thumb drive to give to our MUFON Director of International Investigations, Robert Spearing, since he was working to combine them so the presentation would transition smoothly between his portion of the presentation and mine. As I approached him outside of the conference room to check on his progress, all of the media that was embedded in the slideshow disappeared. I saw a look of bewilderment flash across his face as he explained what happened. I stood there with him and quickly tried to think of solutions such as restoring a previous version of the slides. Nothing was working to fix the problem. After about ten minutes of this, he turns to me and says, "You are an experiencer, are you not?" "Yes, a Near-Death Experiencer. Why?" He then told me to leave, which I did, not fully understanding why he had directed me to do so at the time.

Approximately an hour later, I saw Robert again, this time up and walking through the commons area outside of the conference room. I asked if he was able to get the slides fixed and he told me, "You are not going to believe this. As soon as you walked away all of the media just reappeared without me having to do anything." The implication was clear, I then realized that my high level of anxiety had probably once again interfered with the electronics, just as it had done with my Zoom calls and my microwaves. The Cases of Interest

114

presentation ended up going off without a hitch and it was a wonderful way to end the symposium that year. Although the electrical malfunctions continue around me to this day during times of high emotion, I am hopeful that as I continue to grow as a person and conquer my fears by challenging myself to experience new firsts, my anxiety will decrease and it will, in turn, reduce the frequency and severity of this aftereffect.

Around this same time, I had begun working with a small team of members from MUFON leadership to revamp some of the forms which we used in our UFO investigations. This was to be a first step in updating our organization and working to build a better training platform for new Field Investigators. We had a website for MUFON University, but the function, look, and content needed a major upgrade, so our team worked tirelessly to create a more intuitive experience for those who would be onboarding in the future. This required us to create a new written curriculum as well as film a video training series aimed at walking volunteers through the process of completing a comprehensive UFO investigation.

To our benefit, one of our team members, Teri Lynge-Kehl, along with her husband Kevin Kehl, owned Kehl Media, a broadcasting and media production company. Once several of our new videos were scripted and ready to be recorded, I flew out to Tennessee to join my friend and mentor to begin filming. For two weeks, I stayed in the guest room at Teri's beautiful Victorian Era home while we continued to work on combing through old training materials. In the 1800's the home had been owned by the House of Representatives Speaker General Adkins and they would hold meetings there concerning matters of the state. It had seen wounded soldiers pass through its doors during the civil war, and prior to that, the land had a long history of being a sacred gathering place for local tribes due to the natural spring found on the property. Teri was instantly drawn to the home and its mystique given that she was a member of the clergy and an experiencer herself, having been miraculously healed from a medical condition following an entity encounter. Hers is one of the only documented cases where alien DNA was successfully collected and analyzed following a contact event.

As one might expect, staying in a home that is so spiritually charged, with two major experiencers present, things quickly became interesting. The guest room where I was staying had seen a couple of deaths, but I never did have a run-in with any of the known resident ghosts. One night I did see a small shadow on the floor, and I believed for a moment that one of the Kehl's small dogs may have got trapped in the room, but upon closer inspection I did not find anything in the room to account for what I had seen. Later in my stay, it was revealed that many people have seen that same small shadow darting across the floors in the house.

What happened one of the last nights I was there was something entirely new for both me and for the usual paranormal activity which was common in the home. As I was lying in bed one night looking at my phone and waiting to get sleepy, a bright white light shined into one of the windows. I was up on the second story, and the window which the light was shining in was adjacent to the large balcony where we would sometimes sit and unwind in the evenings. I tried to explain it away as the Kehls possibly playing a prank on me and shining a spotlight into the window from the balcony, but this made absolutely no sense. It was not in their character to do something like that. So, I quickly jumped up and ran to the window to try to get a better look at what was casting this light. As I parted the sheer curtains, all I could see was a blinding white light directly out in front of the window, maybe a foot away. I could not tell what kind of object it was emanating from, only that it was self-contained and located directly outside of the window.

Curious as I was about it, I did not decide to go out on the balcony to further investigate, and I did not choose to go wake the Kehls to get them involved. Instead, in a fashion we see all too often in these types of encounters, I calmly walked back to the bed, laid down, and returned to looking at my phone until I fell into a deep sleep. Sometime later in the night, I awoke to find myself holding my phone up towards the ceiling in a manner that I would if I were looking at the screen. The brilliant white orb of light measuring approximately a foot in diameter was now hovering a couple of feet below the ceiling, centered over my right side at the foot of the bed. In response, I did not take a picture like you would expect an investigator would do. Incredibly, I calmly shut off my phone, turned over, and went right back to sleep. As previously shared, I have witnessed lighted orbs in my home following my NDE, but this orb was very different. It was much larger and brilliantly radiant, shining so brightly that a starburst pattern of light emanated from its core. It was evident to me that this orb of light was something altogether different from all the ones I had witnessed previously in my lifetime.

The next morning, I shared my experience with Teri, and she relayed that she had not had any reports of this type of encounter in her home before. I did not notice any abnormal markings on my body or feel any fear in response to the event, so we made note of the strange happening and moved on with focusing on our work. I was going to be heading back to Oklahoma the next day, so we needed to make the most of our time while I was still there. That night I began packing up my suitcases and getting everything situated since we were going to have to leave at 2 AM to make the two-hour drive into Nashville in order to reach the airport in time for my scheduled departure. Around

10 PM I gathered up my toiletries and headed to the restroom to take a quick shower before turning in for a short night of rest. As I was heading that way, I stopped at the top of the grand staircase to chat with Kevin about my visit. He made mention of the fact that the resident spirits had seemed to be relatively quiet the whole time I was there, to which I replied with something of the sentiment of, "Maybe they just really like me." We had a good chuckle, then I proceeded on to the restroom to take my shower.

As I was stepping out of the bath and drying off, I started to notice what I thought was a rhythmic beeping. At first, I assumed it may have been a timer or alarm clock going off in another room. It was hard for me to determine exactly what the noise could be since I had taken my hearing aids out and left them in the bedroom while showering. As I listened intently trying to determine what it was that I was hearing, I started to realize that there was some type of commotion going on somewhere out on the second floor. I quickly got dressed and went to investigate. Once in the hallway, I passed by Teri's room, and she anxiously motioned for me to come in and speak with her. She explained that the smoke alarm located in the bedroom where I had been staying started alarming while I was in the shower, and at first, they could not locate it in the room. After some searching, she and Kevin were able to find it and disarm the alarm. After a thorough examination of the unit and batteries, they could find no reason why it had started alarming. I chose to see it as a comical response to our earlier conversation on the stairs, and a final farewell before I headed back to Oklahoma. Following that day, frequent unexplained activity resumed in that bedroom after my departure, but the Kehls report no further disturbances from that smoke alarm.

Once I had returned home, I resumed my hard work to revamp the curriculum at MUFON University and busied myself with my other duties aimed at further developing the Oklahoma State Chapter. During this time, I continued to overwhelmingly experience a few of the more amazing aftereffects which have remained so prominent in my life following my NDE. Although they are often broken down into separate phenomena in most literature on the subject, I have always experienced them as presenting in an intertwined fashion where it is hard to separate any one from the whole. Listed separately they are: Having a sense of timelessness where you understand the big picture; remembering the future; and having a new life purpose where life seems to happen for you, not to you.

Although the word afterglow is often used to describe a radiance which remains after a successful or happy experience, I feel it is a fitting word to use for what I have continued to experience in my life following my brief sojourn through the Void. What I had once considered as almost certainly unobtainable for a quiet housewife from Oklahoma instantly transformed into an easy reality for me in the matter of only a few years. Upon my return to this reality, I have always carried with me a new, deeply ingrained understanding of the connections and timelessness of our existence here on this Earth. I now understand how I can reach back in time and supply unconditional love, understanding, and support to my younger self and this immediately manifests into my current reality. Likewise, I can listen for guidance from my future self and receive this knowledge into my life now. This experience of the intricate connection throughout all stages of my existence is what has allowed me to walk through the life path which is now laid out for me. It also allows me to connect with things yet to come through a phenomenon that some refer to as "knowing the future."

The best way that I can explain the way I experience "knowing the future" is by using the analogy of re-watching an old movie.

Imagine it. You are snuggling up on the couch with your spouse and a big bowl of popcorn one evening. As a surprise, your sweetheart has already picked the movie for tonight. It is one from the late 1990s, and although you think you may have heard of it before, you are pretty sure you have never seen it. You start the movie and after about 30 minutes of watching, none of the actors or scenes look familiar. Suddenly, the movie gets into the heart of the action, and you start questioning if maybe you have in fact seen this movie sometime long ago. In a strange sense of detecting some familiarity, you find that you are easily able to predict upcoming scenes. As it turns out, you have seen this movie before, but you are only able to connect with small portions of it in your memory. This is very similar to the feeling I get when I am "remembering my own future." I may not know all the information surrounding the large events which will affect me personally, but I can sometimes tell if something is in my future or not because I can remember it happening to me later in my life. I had this sense very strongly with one of the recent achievements of which I am most proud.

The way my life has taken on new purpose and has been laid out for me following my Near-Death Experience is nothing short of incredible. This is not to say that it all happened without a lot of hard work on my end. Opportunities have been extended to me which have guided my path, but I am responsible for taking the necessary steps to advance down that path. Many times, these steps have been difficult for me due to my ongoing physical impairments and related anxiety, but I choose to step out in the faith that I am following the life course which I was sent back to follow. Synchronicities and coincidences have played a large role in directing my course thus far.

As fate would have it, I happened to live in one of a few states where MUFON needed a complete chapter rebuild when I joined. This was a major reason why I was able to quickly move up the ranks from Field Investigator to State Director. In most other states, this process is something that could take years and years to accomplish. I also joined at a time when the Experiencer Resource Team was undergoing major changes and was looking for new members. This played a vital role in my ability to work directly with UFO experiencers, many of whom had also had an NDE. While attending my first MUFON International Symposium in Las Vegas during August of 2021, I ended up becoming friends with a wonderful group of people from within the ranks of MUFON leadership. Having been some of the warmest and most supportive people that I have met in my lifetime, they welcomed me to join them for dinner that first evening despite my status of being a no-name newcomer.

As we sat and chatted over appetizers, one of the women whom I had not yet met stopped the conversation to tell me that she needed to tell me something. That something turned out to be that as she had been sitting there watching me, all she could see and hear around me was the word "BOOK." Not knowing how well respected and trusted she was as a psychic, I thanked her, then shook it off and continued my conversation. Again, she stopped me and told me more sternly, "You have to write the book!" This time I took note. Just a few hours earlier that day while listening to the main stage presentation by Colonel John B. Alexander, a man who had investigated both UFOs and NDEs in an official capacity, I had leaned over to my husband John and mentioned that maybe I should write a book. What you are reading now is the direct result of that chain of events where I was quite literally guided on my path to write the book.

In the time that followed, more uncanny events unfolded. I had appeared as a guest on several different podcasts, but on one, I spoke more deeply about my NDE and how it led to my investigations into the UFO phenomenon. Unbeknownst to me, one of the MUFON Board of Directors, Teri Lynge-Kehl, was listening. It was that podcast that kicked off our close friendship. Before that time, I had only spoken to her briefly on the phone about official MUFON business, but we never really got to know each other. That all changed following that podcast. She ended up calling me that evening and we talked for over six hours. It felt like I had found a long-lost sister.

As we talked, we realized that we had unbelievably had many of the same type of life experiences. I am convinced that if there are different molds which people are cut from, we most certainly were cut from the same one! As our friendship grew, we of course spoke about many of the things which could be upgraded within MUFON. One of those things was our training platform at MUFON University. For years she had been wanting to upgrade our reporting forms as well as the curriculum found at MU, and I shared that same vision to bring major updates to the organization. With the approval of the Board and our Executive Director, Teri and I began work to update the platform and by the end of the year, I was officially named Dean of MUFON University. It is a title that came with the help of an amazing team of dedicated individuals in leadership at MUFON, and it is one which I carry with much pride. The ability to help standardize training for all Field Investigators to a high level of achievement across the board is one of my most treasured accomplishments thus far!

As I continued to work hard, it seemed that my new life purpose brought new opportunities to me in a steady stream of progress at a level I was able to physically handle. It was almost like a melody, the way my life seemed to be orchestrated by some unseen hand, following the ebbs and flows of my ability. Podcasts, magazines, and documentaries all seemed to find their way to me at times when I was feeling well enough to take them on. Even my case work remained surprisingly manageable with a mixture of cases ranging in response level. In 2021, I received one case which would serve to springboard my Ufology career into the spotlight. It was a case which came to be known as the Miracle Mountains Schoolyard Encounter.

During the fall of 1975, a group of young children at a boarding school in Hartshorne, Oklahoma witnessed a large saucer shaped craft silently approach their location. It flashed multi-colored lights around the perimeter as it slowly descended over a grove of trees on the school property. Becoming fearful for the safety of the women and younger children, the eldest boy present grabbed his rifle, climbed onto the roof of the schoolhouse, and steadied it at the UFO. At this, the object turned onto its side and shot off into the direction of the old sawmill about a mile away. As the children were running into the house, the teacher and a couple of the oldest children remained outside and watched as the object shot out small lighted orbs which danced around in the air before shooting off into the sky. All witnesses remember the events of that day unfolding over the course of over an hour. All remember it being daylight when they first noticed the object, and the full darkness of night as the encounter ended.

Following the initial encounter, there was a wide range of differences in the memories of the witnesses. The children remember returning into the house and having a relatively normal evening, while the teacher remembers much more detail about what transpired throughout the night. She recalls the children being terrified following the encounter and hiding under their beds. During the night, some of the children complained about seeing shape shifting entities outside of the window so the teacher gathered the children in the living room by the fireplace while the eldest boy worked to board up the windows and doors. Grabbing his rifle once again, he stood guard throughout the night until the group could hear the return of the usual sounds of the locust and cattle in the nearby pasture, and they could tell the encounter was over.

The next day, the teacher packed up sack lunches and took a group of the children out for a field trip to search the area of the sawmill for any signs of what had transpired the night before. Although they were unsuccessful in locating anything out of place, upon returning to the school, it was discovered that the outside meat freezer had been emptied of two sides of processed beef during the night. Stranger still is the fact that this meat was returned a day later. Unsure of the safety of the food, the owner of the school hauled all the meat out into a field and burned it, refusing to let anyone eat it. This represents the only case I have personally come across where processed beef was tampered with during an encounter, while the nearby livestock were left untouched. This case has several more facets to it which I will not go into here, but it was found to have many similarities to other well-known schoolyard encounters such as the Ariel School Encounter and the Westall School mass sighting.

The importance of this case due to the large number of witnesses as well as the setting in which the encounter took place, landed it as the 2021 MUFON Case of the Year and I presented my findings at the 2022 MUFON International Symposium in Denver, Colorado. Following this, I was asked to appear on the History Channel's hit TV show, Ancient Aliens for an episode highlighting MUFON's diligent work to find the truth behind the UFO phenomenon. When I first received the email from the producers, I experienced the most overpowering sensation of "remembering the future" which I have had to date. Before I even began sharing the email out loud to John, I prefaced it with, "This is happening!" I had received offers to be involved in other productions before, but they had never followed through. This was the only one where I had that instant memory of being on the show and what the episode would look like. Working with the crew was a wonderful experience, and shortly afterwards I was also invited to take part in a panel of experts at the 2023 Alien Con.

These are things which I could have only dreamed of as a child and never would have believed were possible for me as an adult. I am still unsure if this after effect is part of a universal plan for me resulting from my NDE, or if these things are a direct result of the transformative change in mindset I encountered after working through the distressing aspects of my experience. It may be that the two are one in the same, or they could be two parts of a whole. Regardless of their origin, the fact that I have had these opportunities following a serious medical emergency and have thrived in the resultant weakened state still amazes me every day, and I will be forever grateful for the things I am able to experience while still residing on this side of the veil.

I believe these aftereffects seen in both UFO and Near-Death Experiencers are some of the best evidence that can be used to reveal the authenticity of the experiences reported by those encountering these types of phenomena. In Ufology we are taught to calibrate each witness at the beginning of the interview in order to gauge their beliefs and preconceptions going into a sighting. For those who have had a Category 3 UFO/Entity contact event, it may be beneficial to recalibrate the witness after six months, and again after a year to track any major changes in beliefs and behavior. As revealed countless times by experiencers throughout the ages, when one encounters such an event that serves to change or to unquestionably confirm their perception of reality, they cannot help but be permanently changed by it. These after effects inspire us and drive us to find answers in the face of ridicule and scorn. We cannot claim ignorance any longer. We know without a doubt that there is more to this existence, and we will continue to press on until the truth is revealed: the truth that we are not alone.

Chapter 8

Facing the Void

"One does not become enlightened by imagining figures of light, but by making the darkness conscious."

- Swiss Psychiatrist Carl Jung

Now that I had a better understanding of why I was able to experience my NDE and come away with my memories of the encounter fully intact, as well as why I had undergone such substantial changes following my NDE, it was now time to turn my attention to the setting of the encounter itself. Why had I ended up in such a dark, isolated location, and what did my appearance there mean about the state of my innermost character? After more than four years had passed, I felt that I was finally ready for it. It was now time for me to face the Void.

Not knowing the common term for the darkness I had once encountered, early on in describing my experience, I referred to the place as "the dark abyss." It seemed a very fitting description for where I had found myself, but to decrease confusion, I have now adopted the most commonly used term "The Void." Starting off, I was frightened to begin my journey into understanding the place because I was scared to find out what it may mean about me, about my character, and my ultimate fate. I knew this process would include a lot of soul searching, honesty, and shadow work. I also knew that researching the place was the only way I would ever begin to gain an understanding of what had taken place, and only then could I begin to heal from the trauma that had resulted.

First, I wanted to better understand who was having distressing NDEs. Was there any aspect of my past or of my character which primed me for this type of distressing experience? For this, I turned to one of the leading authorities on the subject, the International Association for Near Death Studies. From their website IANDS.org:

> "NDEs are "equal opportunity" experiences. People from many cultures and backgrounds, and of all ages—from infants (describing their NDEs once they could talk) to elderly people—have had NDEs. NDEs have been reported by males and females, people from all levels of education, of all religions as well as people not involved in any religion or spiritual practice, people of all social/wealth levels, heterosexuals and homosexuals, people with a variety of belief systems including various beliefs about life and death, people with a life history of "good" or "bad" actions, and people with and without mental illness. None of these aspects of a person has made it possible to predict who will or won't have an NDE, or whose NDE will be pleasurable or distressing. (IANDS, About NDEs, 2023)"

This statement echoed what I was finding to be true through attending the IANDS NDE sharing groups. One aspect I found quite interesting in speaking with other experiencers was that those who had endured several NDEs sometimes had vastly different experiences each time. Someone facing a life-threatening chronic illness may find themselves repeatedly brought to a near-death state, only to first encounter Heaven, followed by a second encounter where they suffer a negative judgment, and a third such encounter which lands them in the Void. Incredibly, these vastly different outcomes may be encountered all within the same day!

Next, I turned my attention to learning what information had been discovered specifically about distressing Near-Death Experiences in hopes of gaining a better perspective of why some people have more frightening encounters. Most researchers agree that outside of the traditionally positive NDE, there are four types of distressing NDE which have been identified and are most commonly reported. The first type includes a positive NDE which contains some element(s) that the experiencer interprets as being negative such as a feeling of powerlessness to stop what was happening to them, or encountering beings or imagery which evoked some fear. The second type is represented by encounters such as my own, wherein a person reports experiencing the vast darkness of a limitless void that elicits feelings of despair and isolation. In the third type, the experiencer finds themselves thrust into a hellish landscape where they report seeing other people being tormented, hearing the agonizing screams of others, or encountering evil beings. Finally, in the rarest type of distressing NDE, experiencers describe undergoing a life review wherein they receive a negative judgment by a higher power.

It has been posited that those who were in an anxious or fearful state when dying may be more likely to have a distressing experience on the other side. It is also sometimes put forth that a person's religious beliefs going into this type of encounter can influence what type of experience they may encounter. In this view, if one is primed to believe that they are about to face judgment, then they may be more apt to have a negative experience. Both of these aspects were true of my own experience in that I was highly troubled that my life had been cut short, and once that was accepted, I was instantly focused on the certainty of facing judgment. Other theories about the cause of distressing NDEs place the onus of guilt on the experiencer, calling into question a person's moral character or motives during life, making them the deserving recipients of torment due to a life filled with debauchery, malice, and hate.

I was once on the receiving end of this type of derogatory criticism from an attendee at an online meeting where I was told that since I was a Christian, I had "gotten what I deserved." Thankfully, the facilitator of the group quickly corrected the problem and used the opportunity for a teaching moment. Although it is becoming much more rare, this type of judgmental thinking can be a very real problem for those who have encountered a distressing NDE, as no doubt countless others have endured such uncalled-for scorn and ridicule in the past. Taking into account how difficult it is for those with a positive NDE to come forward and speak of their experiences, it is even more-so difficult for those of us who have walked through literal hell, only to be belittled by these unsympathetic individuals who wants nothing to do with us or our dark musings. It can create an atmosphere which leaves very little room for us to find the same healing available to those with positive Near-Death Experiences. Those of us lucky enough to survive the trauma of our encounters on the other side, sometimes return only to be ostracized and retraumatized by misguided people found within a community where we expected to find some comfort. Instead of much needed compassion, we are often met with further rejection and ridicule. This prejudice permeates through all walks of life including those with deeply held religious convictions, those adhering to more mystical views, and even those within the NDE research community itself.

In her book, *The Complete Idiot's Guide to Near Death Experiences*, author and researcher Dr. P. M. H. Atwater speaks of the unfounded beliefs she has witnessed being held against those who have encountered a hellish, negative, or distressing NDEs:

> "There is no evidence whatsoever that links frightening or hellish experiences with "bad" people or those more fundamental in their religious views. Quite the contrary, such states are encountered most often by ordinary people, many who were family-oriented and active in their communities and business. (p. 25)"

To the full credit of IANDS, their leadership recognized the great need for a focused discussion within the community they were serving and formed a sharing group for those who had experienced a Distressing NDE. As an experiencer, it is very easy to feel isolated and hopeless when you are surrounded by a sea of unbelievers, or believers who cannot relate to your fearful reaction to a dark afterlife, since that was not within their scope of experience. I was able to attend this meeting a couple of times, and although it was a very small group, it was exceptionally beneficial to me to be able to speak freely with those who completely understood the complex emotions, thoughts, and reactions we have following such an encounter. It always helps to know you are not alone, and to hear how others have worked through the same grief you feel. For those who are reading and have endured a Distressing NDE, I highly recommend contacting IANDS to get set up in their sharing group for Distressing Near-Death Experiencers. There are others who understand your situation and can help you in working through it and the difficult emotions which can follow such an experience.

As I continued my research into the known history of these types of encounters, I continually came across the name of one person in particular who was touted to be the foremost expert in the distressing NDE. That person was Nancy Evans Bush. I quickly ordered up her book *Dancing Past the Dark* not knowing what a major impact this book would have on me and my life. For as much as *The Omega Project* helped drive my intellectual pursuits in understanding the connections between the NDE/UFO phenomena, *Dancing Past the Dark* was the one major influence on my journey into examining matters of the spirit to determine what the Void experience meant for me. Being an experiencer of a distressing NDE herself, and quite literally the woman who coined the term, Nancy Evans Bush is President Emerita of IANDS and has researched the Near-Death phenomenon for over four decades.

In the Fall 2009 edition of the IANDS Newsletter titled *Vital Signs*, Nancy was asked to share some of the satisfactions and frustrations she has encountered during her endeavor to expose and explain distressing near death experiences. I am including her response to both sides of the question here, as I believe it excellently illustrates the struggle that endures when it comes to the topic of distressing near death experiences.

"I suppose one satisfaction is that I didn't stop talking just because the topic was unwelcome. The need is so great, and I've been able to say so little. But every once in a while I've heard from someone that my work has helped. That's worth the struggle. And of course, because I didn't stop searching for answers to give to other people, eventually there came a kind of resolution, of understanding, of my own experience. Finally getting beyond the literal interpretation and arriving at a deeper comprehension makes all the difference. And, I keep hoping that some of my conviction is getting through, that we have to recognize that the universe is made up of darkness as well as light, so we'd better pay some attention to the implications of that.

(…) Probably my biggest continuing frustration is the general conviction that if a person has a horrifying NDE, they've done something to deserve it; there must be something about them. No researcher, to my knowledge, has analyzed moral character or previous behaviors to explain radiant NDEs, but an astonishing number of people seem quite sure that a scary NDE is a manifestation of deep-seated guilt, hostility, fear, hatred of God, rigidity, lack of love, meanness, and on and on. No wonder it's been hard for experiencers to come forward to share their difficult NDEs!" (Stringer, 2009, p.4)

It is astonishing that this mindset has continued to permeate the field and remain existent in the community since the 1970s. It is a sentiment that we as a collective have got to get past if we ever hope to quit running from our own fears and begin to pull whatever knowledge we can find from these darker encounters. Until then, we will continue to miss half of the equation!

Another line of thinking that I have personally come across and would like to refute is the belief that a Void type experience is only a "partial NDE." Having been there myself, I am here to tell you there is nothing "partial" about the experience when compared to their more heavenly counterparts. The darker experiences are also not a "lesser" type of experience. Light and dark, positive and negative; they are both valid experiences and each can equally teach us something about ourselves and about our existence. I have heard researchers who claim that positive out-of-body experiences at the point of death constitute a Near-Death Experience, but in the next breath they discount the Void experience as being an incomplete NDE. It is absurd!

As one of the people on this Earth who has actually encountered the Void, I have a very extensive memory of my time on the other side that is complete with all emotions, sights, and interactions. It was ever much as life-changing, and in some instances even more so, than those who had positive Near-Death Experiences in the heavenly realms. Nancy Bush has been speaking about this for decades, but some still refuse to understand or take into account the voices of those who have been to the Void. Just because my tunnel of light didn't appear when I was hoping for it does not make my experience any less important and valuable to the study of Near-Death Experiences or to humanity as a whole. In some ways, the Void experience should elicit more intense study for the fact that it is in opposition to what the majority of the Christian West would expect in the afterlife. Why are some of us having these experiences in a Void that we were not taught about in Sunday School? What does it say about the certainty of the existence of this place, and what more can we learn about it from other traditions around the world?

In the time following my NDE, one of the most important things I did was to turn my attention to deeply understanding the history and traditional thinking surrounding the place I had come to know as the Void. To be perfectly honest, my religious beliefs were in complete shambles for the first few years, not knowing who or what I should trust. Everything I had once faithfully believed had been torn down in a matter of moments during my sojourn into the Void. If I wanted to better understand what had really transpired on the other side, I was going to have to strip away all previous religious preconceptions and be open to understanding other sacred religious beliefs and cultural traditions where truth outside of Christianity may be found. This was a huge step for me, but it was vital to my ability to assess what had truly transpired without any preconceived notions. I now needed to take a step back and listen to what thousands of years of knowledge from around the world could teach me.

Many of the world's religions and creation myths begin with a vast eternal darkness existing before creation when a god or gods begin the process of creating all that we see in existence today. Sometimes these traditions indicate that this dark, wide open void contains water or soil which is then used in building the universe. First turning to the fundamentals of the Judeo - Christian creation account, I reviewed what is one of the more well-known traditions which supports this view. In the New International Version of the Bible, Genesis Chapter 1 Verses 1 - 5 state, "1 In the beginning God created the heavens and the earth. 2 Now the earth was formless and empty, darkness was over the surface of the deep, and the Spirit of God was hovering over the waters. 3 And God said, "Let there be light," and there was light. 4 God saw that the light was good, and he separated the light from the darkness. 5 God called the light "day," and the darkness he called "night." And there was evening, and there was morning—the first day." As we can see, before the Judeo-Christian God created light on the first day, there was only darkness which covered the newly formed earth. He then created light and separated it from the darkness to create night and day.

The ancient Egyptian creation mythology echoes much the same sentiment. It can be found recorded in the Egyptian Book of the Dead, on ancient papyrus texts, and quite literally set in stone amongst the hieroglyphics found inscribed on pyramid and temple walls. In this tradition, all that once existed was a dark expanse of waters called Nun which was described by dividing it into male and female pairs representing the characteristics of the space. These pairings conveyed that the space was a watery expanse, dark, infinite, and wandering. The Sun God Ra, in his pre-creation form referred to as Atum, generated creation out of the Chaos of Nun.

The 7th century Greek Poet Hesiod detailed the Greek creation myths in his poem Theogony. In this, the beginning is described as Chaos, a divine, empty void. From the personified location of this limitless and formless chasm first Nyx, a dark winged bird, then all else including Gaia, Tartarus, and Eros was created. In Greek culture at the time, Greek philosopher Anaximander wrote of Aperion which he used in order to rationally describe the origin of the universe. This he characterized as the boundless existence of the ultimate reality. His cosmological theory puts forth the idea that there exists an infinite source from which all in existence is derived and is ultimately returned to.

Likewise, the Hindu creation story features an expansive sea of darkness existing prior to the formation of the Earth. From the sacred text The Vishnu Purana:

> "Whilst he (Brahmā) formerly, in the beginning of the Kalpas (a vast cosmic period of time), was meditating on creation, there appeared a creation beginning with ignorance, and consisting of darkness. From that great being appeared fivefold Ignorance, consisting of obscurity, illusion, extreme illusion, gloom, utter darkness."

The examples are endless and originate from all over the world, across different times, cultures, and traditions. In addition to these noted creation stories, there are countless references which can be found referring to dark places existing as instruments of judgment or spaces of self-reflection in the afterlife. The Christian Bible speaks of outer darkness. "But the subjects of the kingdom will be thrown into outer darkness where there will be weeping and gnashing of teeth." (Matthew 8:11-12). So too, the Church of Jesus Christ of Latter-day Saints teaches of outer darkness where those who performed evil works will be cast. The Roman Catholics have the teaching of purgatory, an interim place of purification for God's elect. In the same vein, some Jewish beliefs teach of a time of purification following death. Somewhat in contrast to these, but most consistent with my experience of the Void is the view found in the Tibetan Buddhist Book of the Dead, or the Bardo Thödol. From this viewpoint, the Void is not a place of judgment, but instead, it could denote a place of ultimate Nirvana. According to LāMa Kazi Dawa on *The After—Death Experiences on the Bardo Plane*:

> "At the moment of death, the empiric consciousness, or consciousness of objects, is lost. There is what is popularly called a 'swoon', which is, however, the corollary of super—consciousness itself, or the Clear Light of the Void; for the swoon is in, and of, the Consciousness as knower of objects (Vijnāna Skandha). This empiric consciousness disappears, unveiling Pure Consciousness, which is ever ready to be 'discovered' by those who have the will to seek and the power to find It.
>
> That clear, colourless Light is a sense—symbol of the formless Void, 'beyond the Light of Sun, Moon, and Fire', to use the words of the Indian Gitā. It is clear and colourless,

but māyik (or 'form') bodies are coloured in various ways. For colour implies and denotes form. The Formless is colourless. (Wentz, 2000, p. 93)"

A state not of eternal suffering, but of Ultimate Reality for the existence of pure consciousness. Although my existence was one of personal torment due to the distress I was experiencing from the loss of my earthly life, now that I am removed from the environment and can detach myself from the emotions I was experiencing at the time, this is the view of the Void which sits right with my soul at a very fundamental and primal level. The Void itself did not extend any ill will towards me, but instead had offered me a place free of influence to purge and to feel in the purest state of consciousness. From this, I wondered what others had concluded from their time in the Void, or as the result of other distressing afterlife encounters. I finally allowed myself to read accounts from others detailing their own frightening NDEs.

Turning first to Nancy Bush's account, she describes the distressing Near- Death Experience she had following complications from childbirth which required her to be put under anesthesia. After sailing above building tops and into the vast darkness of space, she witnessed what she was later able to identify as a small group of black and white yin yang circles that taunted her unmercifully. They flew around her and clicked, relaying messages that her existence and everything she loved had all been a big cosmic joke. She was told that none of it was real, and that she herself was never real. The dark existence where she found herself is all there ever was. As the black and white symbols moved off into the darkness, she found herself alone, away from everything she loved, and her spirit was filled with overwhelming grief. In the next instant, she found herself awakening in the hospital, fully aware of what she had experienced. She questioned why God would cast her into darkness, and wondered if the symbols had been right, was any of this real? The doctors, the nurses, and even the baby she had just given birth to, were they real? Although lessening with time, this feeling of existing in a phantasmal world remained with her for years.

It was amazing to hear of someone else having an encounter which included elements so similar to what I had endured both during and after my time in the Void. Upon reading it, I instantly felt a sense of compassion and validation for what I had understood of my own encounter. One point which I continue to find fascinating is that Nancy had an encounter which prominently featured the yin yang symbol which traditionally highlights the contrast between darkness and light, the opposite but interconnected nature of things. How fitting then that she would bring that image back with her into a life that serendipitously found its way into researching and working with Near-Death Experiencers through IANDS. Incredibly, this symbolism has gone on to be a recurring theme in her life's long work in the field, as she has worked tirelessly to bring recognition to the dark as the necessary equal and opposite of the more positive Near-Death Experiences. This duality of positive vs. negative, darkness vs. light, has played out in multiple ways throughout the fields of Near-Death and UFO studies over the years.

One of the most prominent ways in which we see this contrast displayed is in the portrayal of each phenomenon throughout pop culture. Past literature would have you believe that all alien abductions are almost always a negative experience, while Near-Death Experiences are, for the most part, positive. A better understanding and investigation into each of these experiences shows that modern abductees often report positive experiences with these entities, and near-death experiences sometimes report negative experiences while on the other side. It is important to take an honest look at each of these types of encounters while also acknowledging that personal reactions play a large role in our interpretation of the intent and tone of these encounters.

I am reminded of a video I once saw online of an abandoned dog who had been found on the street and brought into a shelter for treatment. A full-grown adult dog, it was severely thin and frail and in desperate need of nourishment and veterinary care. The problem was that it was so frightened that it backed into a corner and yelped uncontrollably any time a well-meaning caretaker approached it. I had come across this video only about a year after my VAD and I remember sitting there heavily sobbing because I felt so much like that terrified animal who did not understand what was happening to him. He experienced such terror from those who only wished to help him, but he did not understand what they were trying to do. He was getting in the way of his own salvation. I wondered if my fear in the Void was a reflection of what I was seeing this poor dog go through. As a human with the knowledge that these people had the ability to save and comfort this desperate animal, it was heartbreaking to watch as he yelped and cowered from what he no doubt had come to believe about humans. I cannot help but wonder, if this is what the unknown male presence went through watching me while I was so terrified in the Void. There is little doubt that our expectations and past experiences play a role in how we interpret such supernatural encounters.

Revisiting the Kelley - Romano Study on UFO Experiencers, one of the defining characteristics they determined to be related to UFO abductions is the prevailing belief that such an encounter would be negative in nature. This can be easily understood when viewed against our American pop culture and the way Hollywood has classically portrayed alien encounters on the big screen. Movies such as *The Day the Earth Stood Still, War of the Worlds,* and *Earth Vs. The Flying Saucers* all present an "us against them" rivalry in a battle for the survival of mankind. Even movies based on true events such as *Fire in the Sky* detailing Travis Walton's days long disappearance following a UFO encounter in the Sitgreaves National Forest evoked a feeling of great fear. Is it any wonder our population is primed to believe that any such encounter would be unequivocally negative?

The Cambridge Dictionary defines abduction as "The act of making a person go somewhere with you, especially using threats or violence," so it is not hard for one to understand why using such terminology would lend to a negative perception of the phenomenon. Despite this, only 20.8% of the 2006 Kelley - Romano survey respondents reported having a negative UFO contact experience. This seemingly counterintuitive result has been repeated time and time again through studies carried out by different organizations including the Dr. Edgar Mitchell FREE Foundation and MUFON's Experiencer Resource Team, where abductees have continued to report having predominantly positive experiences despite having an initial fear-based reaction to the phenomenon. This finding resulted in the UFO research community largely turning away from using negative leaning terminology such as "abductee" and replacing it with the more neutral term "experiencer." In their 2018 research survey, The Dr. Edgar Mitchell FREE Foundation found that of 1,534 respondents reporting a physical contact experience with a non-human intelligence, 66% viewed their experiences as "Mainly Positive," and 29% viewed their experiences as "Neutral." Only 5% of respondents to their survey reported their experiences as "Mainly Negative," pointing to the possibility that public perception of the phenomenon is starting to shift as the topic continues to become increasingly destigmatized in the mainstream and as more experiencers have come forward to share their encounters.

On the opposite end of the spectrum, we have the overwhelmingly positive portrayal of Near-Death Experiences in dominant mainstream culture. Movies such as *Heaven is for Real, 90 Minutes in Heaven, Miracles from Heaven, and The Boy Who Came Back from Heaven* all point to the media bias on the subject. And who can blame them? The truth is, Heaven sells. Nobody wants to go to the movies and be reminded of the fact that there may be other options as to what could happen to them after their Earthly life is over. The Void and other Hellish afterlife encounters just do not give people the same warm fuzzy feelings that visions of Heaven evoke. Although they are few and far between, there are others who have braved the possible ridicule to come forward and publicly share their not so pleasant Near-Death Experiences. One of the most well-known distressing encounters comes from Art Professor Howard Storm.

An atheist at the time of his encounter, Storm suffered a perforated bowel during a June 1985 trip to Paris with his wife and students. While at the hospital waiting for the arrival of the surgeon who was to perform the needed surgery, he lost consciousness and found himself standing outside of his body. As he was observing his wife crying by his bedside, he could hear voices beckoning him out into the hallway. There, he encountered pale humanoid creatures who became hostile and began attacking him when he resisted following them any further. Fearful, he began praying to God causing the creatures to withdraw. Once alone, he called on Jesus to save him and was greeted by beings of light who ushered him through a life review process before being shown visions of a cataclysmic future. Following his encounter, he awoke in the hospital while being prepped for surgery. The encounter affected Storm so profoundly that in the years following, he attended seminary where he obtained a Master of Divinity degree and became an ordained minister.

According to estimates put forth by Dr. P.M.H. Atwater, as many as 15 percent of adult Near-Death Experiencers have had distressing encounters such as what Storm endured, although some estimates put that number as low as only 1 percent. It is difficult to obtain accurate numbers on the true occurrence rate due in part to the reluctance of those who have had such distressing encounters to come forward and share their stories. Despite this, those who have reported having a negative NDE, later report being able to integrate the encounter into their lives in a positive manner. This pattern can easily be seen in the examples we have discussed in this chapter. Bush used her encounter to further research and understanding of distressing NDEs while Storm went into the ministry as a result of his encounter. Even my own journey produced positive results as I turned to using my encounter as a guide for helping those experiencing distress and/or a sense of powerlessness resulting from their UFO/UAP contact encounters.

Another often overlooked duality is the occurrence of "dark" aspects which can result from even the most positive NDE. Although these unpleasant precursors and after effects are recognized as being part of the phenomenon, it is a side of the NDE which many experiencers do not wish to discuss, and for good reason. As we will see, it is not all sunshine and rainbows leading up to and following a near death experience. There is a shadowy yin to the light of the NDEs yang. In Chapter 6 of this book, we looked at some of the negatives associated with the encounter prone personality including childhood trauma and abuse. In Chapter 7, we looked at many of the related positive outcomes that I personally experienced as a result of my NDE. Here, I would like to examine some of the resulting negative characteristics of the NDE which include the ongoing social and spiritual issues that all Near-Death Experiencers face to varying degrees.

Many of these difficulties are the result of the known divide NDErs instinctively place between the former and current self. Some have problems reconciling their previous religious beliefs with new convictions gained as a result of their experiences on the other side. A person like myself who may have once held strict fundamentalist beliefs, can see those go out the window in an instant as they emerge from their encounter carrying a more liberal and inclusive view of religion. Loved ones struggle to relate to what is now an almost unrecognizable NDEr with whom they once shared similar values and beliefs. As the NDEr struggles to cope with the mental and spiritual changes they have undergone, relationships can deteriorate to an irreparable extent resulting in a known divorce rate of 75% following a Near-Death Experience. In his paper titled *NDEs as the Focus of Clinical Attention* which was featured in The Journal of Nervous and Mental Disease, Dr. Bruce Greyson states:

> "Because many of their new attitudes and beliefs are so different from those around them, NDErs can overcome the worry that they are somehow abnormal by redefining for themselves what is normal. NDErs may feel a sense of distance or separation from people who have not had similar experiences and may fear being ridiculed or rejected by others - sometimes, of course, with good reason. Difficulty reconciling the new attitudes and beliefs with the expectations of family and friends can interfere with maintaining old roles and lifestyle, which no longer have the same meaning. NDErs may find it impossible to communicate to others the meaning and impact of the NDE on their lives. Frequently, having

experienced a sense of unconditional love in the NDE, the experiencer cannot accept the conditions and limitations of human relationships. (Greyson, 1997, p. 327-334)"

Dr. Greyson goes on to argue that these resulting characteristics should not be viewed as indicative of mental illness, but should instead be considered as part of a natural response to an extremely stressful situation. Just as one would expect a period of grief and depression following the loss of a loved one, these actions and emotions reflect a person who is reacting naturally to a life-threatening event. However, it is acknowledged that some Near-Death Experiencers who encounter severe difficulties in coping with the emotional, spiritual, and social fallout of their encounter may be diagnosed with PTSD or Post Traumatic Stress Disorder. In my own experience, a diagnosis of complex PTSD was a significant step that allowed me to begin processing what had occurred and understand how to best integrate the event into my new reality.

In recognizing that these sometimes-negative aspects which I had been experiencing were part of the natural and expected healing process following a NDE, I was able to be gentler with myself and my feelings towards what I had endured physically, mentally, and spiritually. I found that despite the initial feelings of isolation and fear, the gradual generation of compassion and self-love were also natural reactions to my experiences in the Void. In beginning to accept these changes I was undergoing as a result of my long journey, I discovered that there was an unexpected solace to be found in the shadows.

I believe there is a great need to find balance in the darkness so that we may clearly discern what these phenomena are trying to tell us, as opposed to observing only that which we have been primed to hear. While darkness can sometimes conceal great horrors within its shadows, the darkness of a mother's womb offers nourishment, protection, and ultimately brings forth new life. Likewise, light can produce positive or negative scenarios as it can be used to purify, but close or prolonged exposure may result in getting burned. New beginnings spring forth at the light of day, but deep restoration takes place during the still darkness of the night. There is a simple beauty to the natural balance and endless lessons to be found on either side. Just as the monistic dualism of the yin yang, both darkness and light are the necessary components of a unified reality where the hidden netherworld of the Yin and the overt worldliness of the Yang join in perfect harmony to illuminate extraordinary hidden truths.

Chapter 9

Source Reality, the Gateway Process, and the Cosmic Hologram

"We might be the holographic image of a two-dimensional structure."
- Theoretical Physicist Brian Greene

One of the more interesting aspects of my encounter into the Void took place in the time directly following my return to this plane of existence. Despite the unrelenting physical pain that I experienced the first two years subsequent to the artery dissection, I struggled heavily with reintegrating my mind and spirit back into this world. As a result of my sojourn to the other side, I had brought back with me the knowledge of an ultimate reality where creation exists in its purest state, outside of the confines of time or construct. I found that this physical world offered only a mere glimmer of what we are truly meant to be, and this resulted in an overwhelming feeling of restriction and heaviness in every way. Although I loved my family and was overjoyed to have the opportunity to be back here with them, my mind was in a constant state of dissonance as I struggled to reconcile the advanced conscious form I had taken on the other side with the broken, clunky body and existence I now found myself confined to. I was no longer existing in my truest form, and I knew it.

Knowing my experiences to be legitimate, in the spirit of being pragmatic, I would like to address here a very real effect known as derealization which can be triggered by heightened levels of fear, anxiety, and stress. According to the Mayo Clinic, a person experiencing derealization can experience a distorted perception of their surroundings including seeing the world as being two dimensional, experiencing difficulty judging the elapse of time, feeling unfamiliar with surroundings, and feeling disconnected from loved ones. Although fleeting experiences of derealization are common and not cause for concern, severe recurrent episodes which last several months could be indicative of a disorder. Taking this into account, I feel that although I never carried a formal diagnosis, this is a close explanation for what I experienced in the years following my Near-Death Encounter.

Nevertheless, if one considers the events which transpired prior to this, there is a clear reason for the feelings of detachment I had from this reality. These feelings did not arise out of unfounded or delusional belief, but instead, they were the direct consequence of an experience which placed me in a very real place outside of this realm. Disorientation did not grip me, but instead it was the memory of a reality much more real than this one that carried the feelings of detachment into this existence. It is my experience that the symptoms of derealization which did arise following the period of extreme trauma in my life were all founded in the reality of the Void. With this in mind, I would like to turn now to revealing the all-encompassing and pervasive thoughts I experienced directly following my encounter while I was first trying to reconcile my memories of the Void with what I would have considered sane, rational thinking here on Earth. Do these insights reveal a glimpse of the truth behind an ultimate reality, or are they merely the coping mechanisms of a mind trying to process the extreme trauma of a life-threatening medical emergency?

While recently speaking with Laurie about the time I spent at her home, I discovered that although I previously believed that I did not share my afterlife experiences with anyone until much later, I had actually revealed much more about my time on the other side than what I first realized. She revealed that I had begun sharing glimpses of my experience during those very first few days following the NDE. This is something I do not recall doing as there are still some gaps in my memory from directly before and after the event. Laurie shared that starting the first night I was there, we would sit and watch TV into the early morning hours because I was having terrible nightmares relating to my experience. Though exhausted, I would fight sleep due to the overwhelming fear of dying and once again returning to the darkness. As we would be watching a show, she explained that I would pause the television, turn to her, and out of nowhere, I would begin relaying deeply profound things about my time on the other side. She would sit and quietly reassure me while I spoke, and once I was done, I would almost robotically pick up the remote, resume the show, and swiftly fall into a deep restful slumber. She said that I would go on to repeat this procedure night after night for the entire length of my stay.

Although the full magnitude of information that I was able to share during those early days has lessened, I do still retain a strong memory of the main themes that were impressed upon me while there. This download of information was something that was imprinted upon my spirit during my time spent on the other side, and it lingered with me for years after I was reinserted back into my life here on Earth. This type of "information download" is a phenomenon reported by a small subset of cases within the Near-Death and UFO Experiencer communities, and has revealed insights on a variety of different subjects through the various expereincers encountering them. What follows in this chapter is the direct product of my time spent in the Void, and the reader may sense a shift in tone as what was experienced there is well outside of the bounds of my usual, everyday thinking. When I first began sharing these insights with my family, they would sit awestruck at the information coming from me as they knew these were not things I would normally speak about. I now wish that I would have recorded those initial musings which were relayed back then, during the first two years after my NDE.

While exploring my deepest thoughts and innermost memories of the place where I briefly resided, it has occurred to me that although this area is often referred to as the Void due to its absence of all manner of substance and comfort, my experience of it both confirmed and contradicted that description. I felt overwhelmingly that all things existed there in their purest eternal form, their energy radiating with eons of existence and potential within the darkness of the Void. The concept seems to be completely antithetical. How can this place be everything and nothing, without beginning and without end?

It was my experience that everything in existence, across all dimensions, originated from this one ultimate place, our Origin-Point Reality. Upon returning to this Earthly domain, I arrived back here with the perception that our reality was a matrix-like simulation made up of 1s and 0s of coded information configured into the hologram we perceive and reside within. Although I knew my physical surroundings were real, they simultaneously seemed to be nothing more than an illusion. I felt as though the form now housing my consciousness was constructed of some organized collection of cosmic binary designed to fully immerse me into this physical experience. Because of this, the avatar which I donned in order to regain my life here was able to be mended through code manipulation using the combined will of consciousness through practices such as prayer, meditation, and manifestation. Further healing came through the utilization of sound vibrations and code correction using proper food and herbs which were placed in this reality to be beneficial to our physical bodies. Throughout my prolonged physical suffering, I learned that we can not only influence, but ultimately successfully alter our reality through use of our focused consciousness.

In further assessing the Void, I feel it is the ultimate reality from which this holographic domain originates. In this, I speculate that even those Near-Death Experiencers who found themselves in Heaven were sent into another dimension featuring a different holographic simulation in which they were to reside. For those of us who temporarily encountered the Void, I feel that we are the few who got to see behind the curtain of the "Great and Powerful Oz." Once exposed to its infinite magnitude, the overwhelming revelation of this ultimate reality generates feelings of immense awe and anguish as each soul grapples with comprehending all that its existence implies. Just as biblical heroes of old trembled and fell on their faces when in the presence of angels, how much more justified are those common men and women who also found themselves struck with terror while being laid bare before the origin of their own creation. Those quick to negatively judge experiencers who have journeyed to the darkness of the Void, may do well to take a step back to consider the religious traditions we have already examined, as well as the scientific knowledge which also supports the idea that those in the Void were existing in the pure presence of the Ultimate Source.

As outlandish as these thoughts first seemed to be, I knew them to be an accurate representation of what I had experienced and I came to find that they are aligned with some of the biggest theoretical concepts currently being discussed, Holographic Universe Theory and the Simulation Hypothesis. My assessment of the construct of reality based on my time in the Void best reflects the combination of these two current scientific theories. Holographic Universe Theory puts forth the idea that our world is an illusion created by our brains perceiving energy fields and projecting that information out to form the physical universe where we reside. Simulation Hypothesis takes this concept a step further, attributing everything in our existence to being the product of a computer simulation. But what if that simulation consisted of the coded information for a hologram which our brains compute and translate into reality? Our world would then be the result of an advanced, multi-dimensional hologram being expressed through the algorithm of a complex computer simulation utilizing technology far beyond our human comprehension. This view accurately conveys my lingering impression of our existence, and it explains why my consciousness struggled so heavily with reintegrating back into the confines of this world.

It is my belief that the infinite existence found outside of our own simulated environment consists of multiple layers of holographic dimensions leading up to the one ultimate Source Reality where entities may be found residing in their purest, conscious energy form. Many of these various types of energy beings manifest into our realm from the Void, the Origin-Point Reality from which I had emerged following my NDE. Due to circumstances found within the human experience such as possessing naturally in-born abilities, or the development of an encounter prone personality, some of us have an enhanced ability for acquiring an open connection to that realm allowing for the experience of such phenomena including UFO contact, NDEs, and mediumship.

It is a notion which has been pondered by one of the most notable Ufologists in modern history. Speaking from his many years investigating the UFO phenomenon, incredibly, famed French Ufologist Jacques Vallee came to a similar conclusion in his book Forbidden Science Volume 2 where he states:

> "My own working hypothesis is that there exists a parallel reality to which some individuals have access. Whether such access is accidental, deliberate, or by "Invitation Only," I'm not able to decide. The phenomenon provides evidence that our own world is influenced by a higher force acting from that other reality. (Vallee, 1970-1979)"

Could this "higher force" referred to by Vallee be responsible for the genesis of the holographic simulation? As I experienced it, this Originator is an indescribably Immense Force which permeates everything in creation, all while containing the endless possibilities of that creation across infinity. Each individual energy being contained therein is a point that is connected with all else, constituting the whole. And while our simulation readily provides the coded information for the structure of all matter, it seems to lack the information on what each of those structures truly "is." If one removes its physical structure, then tries to define an apple outside of that structure or its relationship to other matter, then what is it? Does the essence of the apple still remain? In much the same manner, I have heard it asked, if you purchase an old boat and in restoring it you end up replacing all of its parts, is it still the same boat? Does the spirit of the original boat still remain when all of its physical attributes are gone, or does it cease to exist? What if we are talking about a human? If we remove the body, does the spirit of the human form still remain?

If one takes the view that we are all spirit beings housed in fleshy constructs, then why would we think it is any different for other entities entering into this reality? Are we wrongly ascribing biological bodies to entities who may not fundamentally possess them? While in the Void, I encountered an entity which, like me, did not appear to have physical form while existing there. Throughout my many years of investigations and interviews with experiencers of varying types of paranormal phenomena, I have come to find that here in our realm, one person's ghost may be another person's alien. To yet another person, the same entity could represent a demon, whereas to another it may be an angel, or even possibly a god or a trickster spirit. I have worked on several cases with people reporting "human-like" beings which were "transparent," but instead of these being reported as ghost encounters, they were reported as alien abduction experiences. Individual interpretations of shadow people by those encountering them range from the demonic to the extraterrestrial. How are we then to assess the sometimes non-physicality of these intelligent beings? Is it possible that these entities are so advanced that they have the ability to project their consciousness into our physical realm with relative ease? And what of their craft? Are some of these non-physical entities responsible for piloting UAP and for the alien abduction/contact phenomenon? It may be as simple as building their avatar and entering the hologram.

As a young child at the time, I can still clearly remember the excitement surrounding the purchase of our first Atari home gaming system. My brother, who was 8 years my senior, was the one in charge of all the electronics since he was the one who best understood the groundbreaking technology of such advanced devices. We spent countless hours in our back playroom battling each other on classics such as QBurt, Pole Position, Packman, and Pitfall. As we got older, our video game systems advanced quickly throughout the years. Soon came our first Nintendo Entertainment System. We were the first ones to own one on the block, so all of the neighborhood kids gathered on our front porch to watch through the bedroom window as we played Super Mario Bros. Looking back, it is easy to see how much things have changed since the early days of home video game systems. Technology has progressed exponentially to where the realistic qualities of today's graphics are mind blowing by 1980s standards. High-Definition monitors and Virtual Reality headsets have now allowed us to glimpse the first steps into fully immersing ourselves in a simulated reality where our only limits are those programmed into the games by their creators.

Much like the Matrix in which Neo finds himself immersed following his decision to take the red pill offered by Morpheus, our future may be one in which we find ourselves living lives fully immersed in the created worlds which afford us the ability to exist in an exciting new reality. As with most modern video games, we begin by selecting the physical attributes that will best suit our needs in the environment, and ones that best reflect the character we wish to portray. We choose their gender, hairstyle, body build, and sometimes even their backstory. Once we hit start, our avatar now comes to life as we officially enter the game. Ones and zeros are being piloted by our consciousness and a subtle flick of a finger. We have now merged with the matrix.

This entering of the game matrix is the same sense which I experienced upon the return to my body. I felt as if someone had hit the "start" button and I had spontaneously respawned at the place where my character had last fallen. Although my life bar was drastically depleted and I had retained some critical damage, I had the chance to complete the mission and later heal, which is exactly what I did. Six long years later, my mind is finally more fully integrated back into this reality, but most of the time I still feel as if I am in a role playing game (RPG) where I have set waypoints and side missions while retaining the free will to explore the open world on the way to a handful of preset locations which have been predetermined for my life. Along the way, I am joined by others, venturing on their own journey, who have donned their avatars and are determined to finish the game. So why are we all here? It could be simply because we wanted to be here! We have chosen to enter this simulated hologram for the sake of having the experience, just as we currently do with our virtual reality video games here on Earth. It is fascinating to think that when we enter those games, we essentially become simulations housed in simulations, each fractal immersing in ever deeper layers, all pointing back to the one true originator.

Just as those virtual characters are functioning within the bounds of the limited knowledge encoded into their world, so too are we typically limited to the information contained within our reality. Considering this, what information may we find coded into our existence, and where could it have come from? In the 2011 NOVA Documentary titled "Fabric of the Cosmos: What is Space?" Theoretical Physicist Brian Greene takes a deep dive into these questions and explains the scientific evidence pointing to the fact that our universe may indeed be a simulated hologram. While this theory points to a significant departure from our conventional understanding of space and reality, Greene explains that the idea can now be supported by evidence derived from a region of spacetime long known for its exceedingly peculiar properties: the black hole.

Traditionally, it was believed that objects, even light, could not escape the intense gravitational pull of a black hole, leading to the assumption that anything thrown into it would be lost forever. However, recent mathematical investigations into black holes have revealed an intriguing discovery. As an object, such as a wallet, falls into a black hole, a copy of all the information it contains appears to spread out and become stored on the black hole's surface, very much akin to how data is stored in a computer. Consequently, while the three-dimensional version of the wallet is trapped inside the black hole, a two-dimensional version persists as information on the surface.

Remarkably, it is now being theorized that the information found on the exterior of a black hole could be utilized to reconstruct any object that entered it. Considering that the rules governing space within a black hole are similar to those on the outside, the implication is that everything in the universe might just be a projection of information existing on some remote two-dimensional plane. Greene summarizes, "If an object inside a black hole can be described by information on the black hole's surface, then it might be that everything in the universe: from galaxies and stars, to you and me, even space itself, is just a projection of information stored on some distant, two dimensional surface that surrounds us. In other words, what we experience as reality may be something like a hologram." (Greene, 2011)

Through the study of quantum physics, we now understand that what was once thought to be an endless sea of empty space, actually contains invisible forces which are fundamental to our existence. This interaction of matter and energy plays out at every level of existence. What are we, but atoms full of empty space, organized and arranged into form, a reflection of what we see in the cosmos. And what of the invisible force of consciousness which sets our reality in motion? In recent history, we, as a society, have overlooked the fact that we exist in both a physical and non-physical, spiritual state. Following the publication of Charles Darwin's book On the Origin of Species, we saw the beginning of the modern separation of science and spirit which has continued to this day. This severance first led to multiple breakthroughs in all fields of science as it was now able to freely operate outside of the strict beliefs and convictions of the church, but this progress ultimately came at a cost. The strict separation of spirit and physical quickly became deeply ingrained in the mindset of our Western society and it has continued to impact our approach to the assessment of non-physical and supernatural capabilities found within our physical world. "The day science begins to study non-physical phenomena; it will make more progress in one decade than in all the previous centuries of its existence." A quote often attributed to the famed Serbian American inventor Nikola Tesla points to the importance of reversing this type of thinking and moving towards a reunification of the two sides in order to advance our knowledge of things which currently seem to be impossible. In a strange set of circumstances, it would be our own United States Government which would end up carrying out such a study.

During the mid -1940s at the height of World War II, US and British forces took part in a focused operation to uncover intelligence relating to the enemy's scientific advances. As part of the Manhattan project, whose aim it was to develop nuclear weapons, the Alsos Mission had a main focus set on detecting and exposing secrets related to the German nuclear program. Not only did the mission accomplish this goal, but it was also ultimately successful in uncovering documents relating to some of the more obscure occult activities being investigated by the Third Reich. In order to stay ahead of our enemy, the US quickly launched its own research into determining the validity and usefulness of such things as Extra-Sensory Perception (ESP), Out of Body Experiences, Remote Viewing, and other methods of psychic intelligence gathering. This analysis probing the bounds of the conscious experience fell under the umbrella of paranormal research in what the Central Intelligence Agency came to refer to as

Phenomenology. From the declassified document titled Brief History of Phenomenology, the study is described as:

> "The investigation of telepathy, clairvoyance, precognition, veridical hallucinations and dreams, psychometry, and other forms of paranormal cognition; of phenomena bearing upon the hypothesis of survival of bodily death; of claims of paranormal physical phenomena such as psychokinesis and poltergeists; the study of automatic writing, trance speech, alterations of personality, and other subconscious processes insofar as they may be related to paranormal processes; in short, all types of phenomena called parapsychological or paranormal. (CIA, 1998)"

Continuing long after the end of the war, research was carried out by various departments within the military and intelligence communities including the Office of Naval Intelligence (ONI), Army Intelligence, and the Defense Intelligence Agency (DIA). One particular study of interest aimed to evaluate the Army's ability to transcend space - time and achieve astral travel in order to carry out intelligence gathering activities. Conducted by the US Army Operational Group under Lieutenant Colonel Wayne M. McDonnell, the analysis of the process focused on a form of brain training which utilized coordinated sound frequencies resulting in what its creator, Robert Monroe of the famed Monroe Institute, referred to as Hemi-Sync. The goal of this Hemi-Sync Technology was to synchronize both hemispheres of the brain in order to facilitate states of consciousness allowing for the expanded awareness of the practitioner. The Army saw use for these expanded states if they could be applied to the creation of psychic soldiers and employed McDonnell to investigate the validity of the technique.

Titled Analysis and Assessment of Gateway Process, the 1983 classified document reported McDonnell's findings resulting from the study to the US Army and Intelligence Command (USA INSCOM) based out of Ft. Mead, Maryland. Declassified in 2003, the report gave a glimpse into the great lengths to which the military was willing to go in order to achieve some of its most unorthodox goals. The strict scientific approach which McDonnell adhered to during the course of the study is evident from the opening paragraph written to the Army Commander wherein McDonnell writes:

"You tasked me to provide an assessment of the Gateway experience in terms of its mechanics and ultimate practicality. As I set out to fulfill that tasking it soon became clear that in order to assess the validity and practicality of the process, I needed to do enough supporting research and analysis to fully understand how and why the process works. Frankly, sir, that proved to be an extremely involved and difficult business. Initially, based on conversations with a physician who took the Gateway training with me, I had recourse to the biomedical models developed by Itzhak Bentov to obtain information concerning the physical aspects of the process. Then I found it necessary to delve into various sources for information concerning quantum mechanics in order to be able to describe the nature and functioning of human consciousness. I had to be able to construct a scientifically valid and reasonably lucid model of how consciousness functions under the influence of the brain hemisphere synchronization technique employed by Gateway. Once this was done, the next step involved recourse to theoretical physics in order to explain the character of the time-space dimension and the means by which expanded human consciousness transcends it in achieving Gateway's objectives. Finally, I again found it necessary to use physics to

160

bring the whole phenomenon of out-of-body state into the language of physical science to remove the stigma of its occult connotations and put it in a frame of reference suited to objective assessment. (U.S. Army, 1983)"

In breaking down his statement, McDonnell divided the investigation of the process into four components which needed to be addressed in order to fully explain why the Gateway experience worked. These elements included the physical aspects, the function of consciousness, the means of accessing the time-space dimension, and the science of the out of body state. All were addressed in the second half of the report following a recap of events leading up to the investigation and the subsequent experimentation of the utilization of the technique. The historic outline included a background on Robert Monroe and his development of the Gateway Process, as well as information on the U.S. Army Chief Warrant Officer Joseph McMoneagle's missions under Project Stargate which primarily focused on remote viewing. McDonnell closed the report by detailing the steps which were undertaken to access the astral realm utilizing the Gateway Process.

Under subsection 11 titled "Consciousness and Energy" of "The Gateway Experience: Brain Hemisphere Synchronization in Perspective," McDonnell delves into the fundamental nature of the material world and reminds the reader that all physical matter is merely the result of the varying energy states of atomic particles. In this, he concludes that "Solid matter, in the strict construction of the term, does not exist." In order for human consciousness to perceive these physical constructs, the energies must interact between the various states of motion vs. rest resulting in the creation of a living pattern projected as a 3D hologram. Although it would be several years before the aforementioned Theoretical Physicist Brian Greene would speak on the possibilities of our world being the projection of data coming from the surface of a black hole, the findings of Lt. Col. Wayne McDonnell seem to support this possibility.

Approaching the subject of our existence in this realm from different angles, concentrated investigation led both men to the same conclusion that our world may merely be a holographic representation of the encoded data stored in cosmic energy fields. This energy passes through the universal hologram and is perceived according to the frequency it conveys in order for the transmission to be interpreted by the human mind. Further theoretical extrapolations suggest that these wave patterns can cross between dimensions where they are received by the human mind's electrostatic field working through a simple binary where it discerns meaning from the coded information by making a series of comparisons.

McDonnell goes on to describe the reasoning behind the ability of human consciousness to transcend the limits of the time - space dimension. In its simplest definition, time is the measurement of energy in motion. The movement of this energy is reliant on its containment within a certain location enabling it to be distinguished from other specific locations in space. Without these boundaries, the energy is infinite, operating outside of the confines of the time - space dimension. McDonnell states, "It is conscious force, the fundamental, primal power of existence without form, a state of infinite being." Although it retains the capacity for consciousness, this infinite force is not part of the universal hologram since it is without limit, without motion, and without form. Energy in this inactive, infinite state is referred to as the "Absolute." Human consciousness has the ability to gain access to these various dimensions located between the physical world and the Absolute. He concludes this section stating,

"Theoretically, human consciousness may continue to expand the horizons of its perceptual capability until it reaches the dimension of the Absolute at which point perception stops because the Absolute generates no holograms of or about itself."

The document goes on to give a detailed account of how human consciousness can transcend the time-space dimension by utilizing the Gateway Process to generate the brain wave frequencies and energy patterns required to escape its bounds. Once free of these constraints, human consciousness can gain access to other dimensions, including details relating to our past, present, and future. Utilizing out of body states such as astral projection, human consciousness "blinking into" the Absolute could return with the newly gained knowledge found far beyond our normal limitations. McDonnell also points out that while separated from the physical, human consciousness can interact with other intelligences found in various dimensions.

Upon release of the declassified Gateway Process report, it was quickly noted that located just prior to McDonnell's final conclusions, page 25 was inexplicably missing from the released document. After several failed FOIA (Freedom of Information Act) requests filed by various agencies and individuals, the document was ultimately released to Vice magazine via an archived copy of the report which had been retained by the Monroe Institute. In it, McDonnell delves further into the meaning of the Absolute in comparison to world religious views and zeroes in on the importance of "Knowing Thyself." He concludes that the act of self-examination prior to undertaking a task such as the Gateway Process is a vital step prior to an attempt to approach the world outside oneself. The evaluation of self is the ability of the holographic consciousness to perceive the form of itself being projected into the universe and being in proper alignment with its own place in the holistic universal hologram. McDonnell viewed the Gateway Process as a portal through which an individual may pass in the process of finding oneself. This application supports my experience of self-reflection which I encountered during my time in the vast expanse of the Absolute Void. My time there resulted in the immediate understanding of the holographic reality in which we reside as well as my place within it.

Ultimately, I believe what Lt. Col. McDonnell attempted to achieve by utilizing the Gateway Process is what I experienced upon the occasion of my temporary departure from this life. Accessing the realm known as the Void, Source, or Absolute, by means such as the states achieved during the Gateway Process enables those who have traversed the infinite magnitude to return with information obtained while in the limitless domain of the Source. In his conclusions of the Gateway report, McDonnell summarizes the applications this practice may have in relation to the objectives set forth by the Department of Defense. He notes in point J that practitioners should, "be intellectually prepared to react to possible encounters with intelligent, non-corporeal energy forms when time-space boundaries are exceeded." This statement further reflects my experiences while in the Void, as I encountered an intelligent entity existing in its pure form who was able to telepathically communicate important information to me. I have no doubt that there is a vast amount of these various types of entities originating from the Source reality which incarnate into this realm whether temporarily materializing or being born here into an Earth native form. Could those entities temporarily visiting our realm be responsible for many of the unexplained sightings which people the world over have been reporting for millennia?

In this, UFO and NDE experiencers are similar since each distinct type of experiencer has been touched by the same energy from the Source reality, either via the location, or the entities which typically reside there. Some UFO Experiencers even indicate that they may have been transported to this Absolute Source reality reporting the perception of a transformation in reality during their encounter. So, what can we extrapolate from Near-Death Experiences in the Void that can be applied to the Ufological field? Just as what was outlined in the Gateway document, these experiences point to the fact that each of us possess a conscious body which exists and can operate outside of our physical body. This body of consciousness can travel into other states of being, including other dimensions, can send information to others instantly via telepathy, and can access information from the Source reality. With future research into the relationship between the physical and conscious bodies and how information is relayed, we may be able to harness this energy for future scientific breakthroughs relating to communications and propulsion systems similar to what was reported to be found in the Roswell craft. The first step we must take is changing the paradigm that science and spirit are mutually exclusive. A deeper understanding of this relationship between the physical and non-physical may lead to breakthroughs in where these craft are originating from, instant communications with the entities originating from there, identification of the technology they are using to emerge into our reality, what their purpose is for visiting our realm, and how we may attain the same capabilities they possess for the betterment of mankind.

What purpose do these types of extraordinary encounters serve in the grand scheme of things? In his Opinion Inventory (OI) of both UFO and Near-Death Experiencers alike, Dr. Kenneth Ring finds that "there is widespread agreement across all groups with statements implying that we are in the midst of an evolutionary spurt towards greater spiritual awareness and higher consciousness and the occurrence of UFO and NDEs is an integral part of that progression."

Could it be that The Source is using these experiences to lovingly remind us of our true calling, worth, and power? As humanity continues to spiral down a self-destructive path, abandoning core spiritual truths for exclusionary reasons, these increasing reminders have been necessary to keep the truth alive for all of humanity. What are these truths? That we are called to love one another, ourselves, and our God. That we are eternal beings who are of The Source. And finally, that we are linked with the power of creation through one mutual spirit to which we will ultimately return.

Like others who have traveled to different planes of existence or those who have interacted with inhabitants of other worlds, my NDE has resulted in my rebirth into a new way of knowing which has affected my entire outlook and understanding of life. No longer do I only have a belief that existence is limitless, for what good is belief when you know something to be true? My spirit has emerged bearing the terrible and beautiful scars gained while wholly experiencing the infinity of being. The battle there within my soul served to burn all of my pride to the ground and a gospel of oneness has arisen in its ashes. The material comforts of the Earth were all exposed to me as a holographic facade. I know now that I am an eternal being, joined with others in love, for it is the only thing which sustains us.

And while the Fabric of Humanity resides deep in the dark cosmos of an unseen dimension, I believe it concurrently exists here on this Earth. It is filled with the loving light extended to us through everyday actions such as a church family opening their home to a friend struggling with unbelievable health issues, a coworker showing abundant kindness to a stranger who desperately needed the help of her expertise, a determined husband who fought through his own fears to comfort and care for his wife, and a child's hug and hand drawn card saying "Get Well Soon Mom." This beautiful kindness was even extended to me by an unknown figure deep in the limitless darkness of the Void. I hope that in some future time I will be granted the gift of seeing his face and given the ability to thank him for the hope he gave me which I still carry with me today. I believe these selfless acts of love collectively form the foundation from which the Fabric of Humanity is constructed. It is woven through all of us, and that love transcends all time and space. Its beauty and glory reside all around us. After all of my torment and all of my trials, the beauty and the pain, I choose to open my heart in gratitude knowing that these extraordinary experiences have served to ground my soul and increase my faith. It is with that same gratitude and understanding that I now wait expectantly to once again glimpse the wonder of the unseen.

Photos

Mindy and family

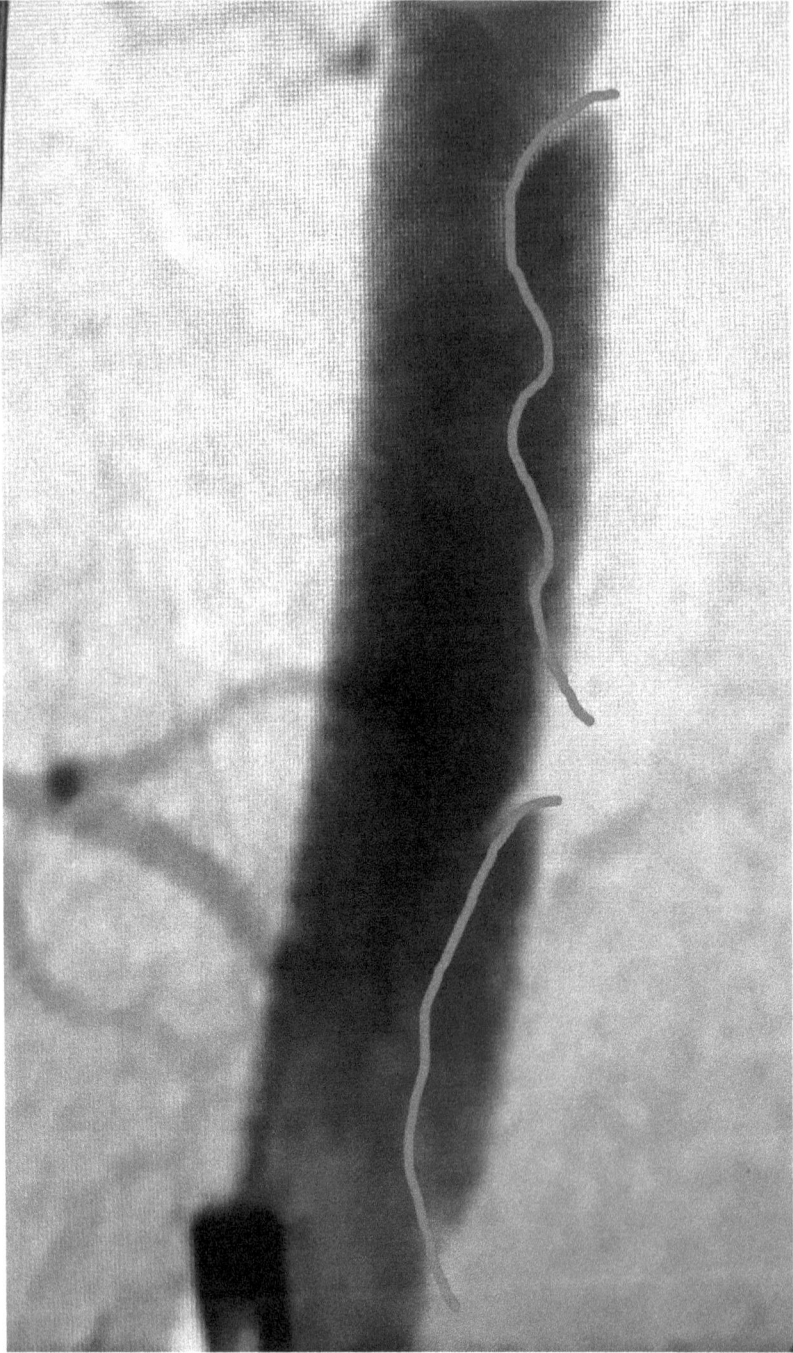

Photo of the aneurysm in Mindy's vein

Suggested Resources

- MUFON - The Mutual UFO Network
  - *www.MUFON.com*
  - Report a UFO Sighting, Entity Encounter, or Abduction Event
  - Suggested resources for Experiencers through the Experiencer Resource Team
- IANDS - International Association for Near Death Studies
  - *www.IANDS.org*
  - Provides resources for Near Death Experiencers including online sharing groups
- NDERF - Near Death Experience Research Foundation
  - *www.NDERF.org*
- *Extraterrestrial Contact - What to do when you've been Abducted* by Kathleen Marden
  - Provides helpful techniques for experiencers who wish to end their contact experiences
- *Dancing Past the Dark* by Nancy Evans Bush
  - Provides in-depth research for those struggling to cope with a Distressing Near Death Experience

About the Author

Mindy Tautfest is a published author, speaker, television personality, and the curator of the Hayden C. Hewes International UFO Bureau (IUFOB). Founded out of Oklahoma City in 1957, the IUFOB most famously investigated the Heaven's Gate Cult, the Aurora Texas Crash and Burial Site, and the massive 1965 UFO Flap over the central United States. Of great historical importance, President Jimmy Carter submitted the original, hand written report of his 1969 UFO sighting to Hayden's bureau, and a copy of the IUFOB report now hangs in the Carter Presidential Library in Atlanta, GA. In 2023, Tautfest recovered the IUFOB files and has been working to digitize and preserve all documents from these incredible investigations.

An Oklahoma native, Mindy got her start while investigating hauntings in the Sooner State in search of answers to her own mystifying experiences. In the past, Mindy has worked as an ICU Nurse with ACLS certification on assignments across the nation and has volunteered her time to Disaster Relief efforts including the Colorado Black Forest Fires, Hurricane Katrina, and the devastating May 3,1999 Moore Tornado. Tautfest now volunteers her time working with the Mutual UFO Network. In this capacity, she serves as the Dean of MUFON University, the Oklahoma State Director of MUFON, and a member of the Experiencer Resource Team. Her investigation of the 1975 Miracle Mountains Schoolyard Encounter was designated as MUFON's Top Case of Interest in 2021, and she was featured on Season 19, Episode 5 of Ancient Aliens speaking about the mass sighting.

In 2016, Tautfest suffered a Vertebral Artery Dissection resulting in a Near Death Experience where she found herself in a place known as the Void. Although traditionally thought of as a separate phenomenon, recent studies have discovered that up to a staggering 55% of UFO Experiencers also report having had a Near Death Experience. This is a little understood statistic, but Mindy's personal encounter with the Near Death phenomenon combined with years of investigations into UFO encounters, places her in a unique position to understand the underlying connections and after effects seen as a result of these enigmatic events. She lives in Oklahoma City with her husband and two kids, JJ and Aneshka, where she enjoys working with experiencers and helping them process these sometimes difficult encounters.

References

Atwater, PMH., (2017)., *After Effects of Near Death States*.
IANDS - International Association for Near Death Studies.
https://www.iands.org/ndes/about-ndes/common-aftereffects.html

Atwater, PMH.,Morgan, D., (2000). *The Complete Idiot's Guide to Near Death Experiences*. Indiana. Alpha Books

Bonenfant, R. J. (2001)., "A child's encounter with the devil: An unusual near-death experience with both blissful and frightening elements ". Journal of Near-Death Studies 20(2), pp. 87-100.

Britt, T.B., Agarwal, S. (2023). Vertebral Artery Dissection. National Library of Medicine.   National Center for Biotechnology Information. StatPearls Publishing LLC.
https://www.ncbi.nlm.nih.gov/books/NBK441827/

Budge, E.A. W., (1898). *The Book of the Dead*. Kegan Paul, Trench, Trubner & Co., LTD . Paternoster House, Charing Cross Road. London

Bush, N.E., (2012). *Dancing Past the Dark: Distressing Near-Death Experiences*. Parson's Porch Books

Campion, T., (2021). *Found: Page 25 of the CIA's Gateway Report on Astral Projection.* Vice Media Group. https://www.vice.com/en/article/v7e4g3/found-page-25-of-the-cias-gateway-report-on-astral-projection

CIA. (1998 Release). *Brief History of Phenomenology.* CIA Reading Room. Document Number (FOIA) /ESDN (CREST): CIA-RDP96-00789R002600310001-9 https://www.cia.gov/readingroom/document/cia-rdp96-00789r002600310001-9

Evans-Wentz. W.Y., (2000). *The Tibetan Book of the Dead: Or The After-Death Experiences on the Bardo Plane, according to LÄma Kazi Dawa-Samdup's English Rendering.* Oxford University Press

Grayson, B., (1997). *The Near-Death Experience as the Focus of Clinical Attention.* The Journal of Nervous and Mental Disease. Volume 185. No. 5

Greene, B., (2011). *The Fabric of the Cosmos: What is Space?* NOVA Documentary. https://www.pbs.org/wgbh/nova/series/the-fabric-of-the-cosmos/

Hernandez, R., (2018). *Beyond UFOs The Science of Consciousness and Contact with Non-Human Intelligence.,* Published in the USA. The Dr. Edgar Mitchell Foundation for

Research into Extraterrestrial and Extraordinary Experiences, FREE, Inc.

Hesiod. (2006)., Theogony ; and, Works and days. Ann Arbor :University of Michigan Press,

IANDS - *International Association for Near Death Studies.* www.IANDS.org

Kelly - Romano, S., (2006). *A Report On the Demographics and Beliefs Of Alien Abduction Experiencers.*, Journal of UFO Studies, n.s. 9, 2006, 1–21© 2006 J. Allen Hynek Center for UFO Studies

Marden, K., (2019). *Extraterrestrial Contact: What to Do When You've Been Abducted.* Newburyport, MA. MUFON an imprint of Red Wheel/Weiser, LLC

Mayo Clinic, *Depersonalization-derealization disorder.* 1998-2023 Mayo Foundation for Medical Education and Research (MFMER). https://www.mayoclinic.org/diseases-conditions/depersonalization-derealization-disorder/symptoms-causes/syc-20352911

Mayo Clinic, *Post Traumatic Stress Disorder.* 2022 Mayo Foundation for Medical Education and Research(MFMER).

https://www.mayoclinic.org/diseases-conditions/post-traumatic-stress-disorder/symptoms-causes/syc-20355967

McDonnell, W.M., (1983). *Analysis and Assessment of Gateway Process.* CIA Reading Room. Document Number (FOIA) /ESDN (CREST): CIA-RDP96-00788R001700210016-5
https://www.cia.gov/readingroom/docs/CIA-RDP96-00788R001700210016-5.pdf

MUFON - *Mutual UFO Network.* www.MUFON.com

Ring, Dr. K., *The Official Website of Dr. Kenneth Ring.*
http://www.kenring.org/

Ring, Dr. K., (1992). *The Omega Project.* New York. William Morrow and Company Inc.

Storm, H., (2008). *My Descent Into Death: And the Message of Love Which Brought Me Back.* Clairview Books

Strieber, W., (1987). *Communion.* New York, Beech Tree Books

Stringer, A., (2009). *Reflections from Three Decades with IANDS.* Vital Signs Newsletter. Volume 28, Number 4

Tucker, R., (2021). *5% have had a near-death experience — and they say it made life worth living.* New York Post

Vallee, J. (1970-1979). *Forbidden Science 2.* The Journals of Jacques Vallee 1970 to 1979. California Hermetica

Wilson, H.H., (2022). *The Vishnu Purana.* Sanskrit Text and English Translation of the Vishnu Purana. Parimal Publication Pvt. Ltd. https://www.wisdomlib.org/hinduism/book/vishnu-purana-wilson

UNXMEDIA

PUBLISHING

Books by Un-X Media

Family Secrets 2017 by Jean Walker
Haunted Independence, Missouri 2017 by Margie Kay
Gateway to the Dead: A Ghost Hunter's Field Guide
2013 by Margie Kay
The Kansas City UFO Flaps 2017 by Margie Kay
The Remote Viewing Workbook 2019 by Margie Kay
A Sonoma County Phenomenon 2020 by Margie Kay
The Color Therapy Wall Chart 1999
The Fast Movers
by Margie Kay, Bill Spicer, and Wayne Lawrence 2020
Doorway to Spirit by Devin Listrom 2020
The Alien Colonization of Earth's Waterways
by Debbie Ziegelmeyer 2021
The Master Dowser's Chart Book by Margie Kay 2022 (lulu.com)
Mandala Meditation Adult Coloring Book by Margie Kay 2023
**Dying to Meet Them: One Woman's Incredible Journey from
NDE to UAP** by Mindy Tautfest 2023
The Unseens by Jeannette LaTulippe 2023
50th Anniversary of the SE Missouri Ozarks UFO Flap
by Debbie Ziegelmeyer and Margie Kay 2023

Un-X News Magazine 2001-2015 and 2001-2023
And coming soon:
More books by various authors and
THOR: The Extraterrestrial on Earth by Margie Kay 2023

Documentary films are in the works.

www.unxmedia.com
Email: editor@unxmedia.com

www.ingramcontent.com/pod-product-compliance
Lightning Source LLC
Chambersburg PA
CBHW072231270326
41930CB00010B/2080